Precious Vessels
of the Holy Spirit

Herman A. Middleton

Precious Vessels
of the Holy Spirit

The Lives and Counsels of
Contemporary Elders of Greece

PROTECTING VEIL PRESS

Acknowledgements:

Special thanks to G. & J. Middleton, P. Navarro, L. Hartung,
A. Taylor, A. & S. Kelpis, V. Petchatnov, P.D. & K.D.,
A. Elliot, I. Piliouris, and P. Becker for their assistance.

Also: The Holy Monastery of Philotheou, Andrew Contes, the Holy
Monastery of Longovarda, Paros, the Holy Monastery of Christ's
Ascension, Drama, Archimandrite I. Argyris, and the Holy Monastery of
St. David, Evia, for their kind permission to include their photos.

In Memoriam: J.V. & J.M. Lewis

PROTECTING VEIL PRESS
Thessalonica, Greece & Asheville, NC
www.protectingveil.com
info@protectingveil.com

ISBN: 960-87614-0-9

Cover Photo: An athonite monk, from the book *Glimpses of the Holy Mountain,*
by the Holy Monastery of Philotheou.

Back Cover Photo: Monastery of the Great Lavra, Mount Athos (Andrew Contes).

All Scriptural quotations for the text are taken from the King James Version. To
better reflect the Greek, we have amended some quotations.

The charismatic phenomena of the first centuries of
Christianity repeated themselves in...monasticism; the elders
were bearers of these charisms - the special gifts of the Holy
Spirit, given to man directly from God....An ascetic is ideally
a God-bearing and Spirit-bearing being....As such he receives
spiritual gifts, an outpouring of which distinguished the first
era of Christianity. The gifts of prophecy, casting out demons,
healing sicknesses, and resurrecting the dead are
not exceptional. They only disclose a normal step
in the spiritual growth of a monk.

- S.I. Smirnov, *The Spiritual Father*
in the Ancient Eastern Church

*For though ye have ten thousand instructors in Christ,
yet have ye not many fathers: for in Christ Jesus I have
begotten you through the gospel. Wherefore I beseech
you, be ye followers of me.*

1 Corinthians 4:15-16

Precious Vessels

The Lives and Counsels of
Contemporary Elders of Greece

Foreword by Dr. Georgios Mantzaridis

Compiled, written, translated from
the Greek, edited, and with a preface,
introduction, notes, and glossary

by

Herman A. Middleton

PROTECTING VEIL PRESS

CONTENTS

Elder Philotheos of Paros at the outset of
his service to the Church, not long after his
ordination to the priesthood on April 22, 1912

PREFACE

> Remember the days of old, consider the years of
> many generations: ask thy father, and he will shew
> thee; thy elders, and they will tell thee.

> Deuteronomy 32:7

> For though ye have ten thousand instructors in Christ,
> yet have ye not many fathers: for in Christ Jesus I
> have begotten you through the gospel. Wherefore I
> beseech you, be ye followers of me.

> 1 Corinthians 4:15-16

This book was initially conceived as a simple anthology of
the sayings and counsels of contemporary Greek elders[1]
who lived and reposed during the twentieth century. Our goal
was not to be exhaustive (there are many great elders who are
not represented here), but rather representative of the spiritual

[1] Elder (in Greek, *geronda*; in Russian, *staretz*): An elder is a spiritually
experienced Christian who, having himself faithfully walked Christ's path to
Golgotha and experienced His resurrection, has thereby experientially learned
the secrets of the ways of spiritual growth. This ministry is administered in a
relationship of complete freedom and love. It is a charismatic ministry that
is often practiced by clergy, although not by any means exclusively.

The history of the Church knows innumerable instances of simple monks, riches which, by God's providence, have been nurtured and preserved even during our age of faithlessness and tragic spiritual decline. It quickly became apparent, however, that for most of the English-speaking world these "voices from the desert" would take on something of a mythological character if they were not accompanied by the lives of the elders, which would put into context and make more real what will seem to many as fantastic accounts and words of counsel that surpass the logical faculties of contemporary man.

Even after writing the lives it became clear that more was needed. We thus decided to preface the lives with a few words of introduction, which present in broad strokes the ancient ministry of spiritual eldership and that introduce the "logic" that puts many aspects of these lives and counsels into their proper context. Finally, we have included a foreword by Dr. Georgios Mantzaridis (Professor Emeritus and Former Chair of the Department of Christian Ethics and Sociology, Theological School of Aristotle University of Thessalonica, Greece). Dr. Mantzaridis masterfully develops one of the most significant presuppositions of the spiritual ministry of eldership, the elder's experience of Christ, Who unites him to all people and to all creation (which is, of course, the goal of every Christian). When the elder experiences and lives the implications of this union, people and creation flock to him, sensing that in his person they will find healing.

laymen, and laywomen who have been shown, through the Holy Spirit, to be faithful spiritual guides. (Please note that uncommon words will be footnoted on their first appearance and not in succeeding appearances. All these words may be found in the glossary at the back of the book).

The goal of reading is the application, in our lives, of
what we read. Not to learn it by heart, but to take it to heart.
Not to practice using our tongues, but to be able to receive the
tongues of fire and to live the mysteries of God. If one studies
a great deal in order to acquire knowledge and to teach others,
without living the things he teaches, he does no more than fill
his head with hot air. At most he will manage to ascend
to the moon using machines. The goal of the
Christian is to rise to God without machines.

- Elder Paisios the Athonite

Elder Amphilochios of Patmos soon after
his ordination to the diaconate on 27 January 1919

INTRODUCTION

It is not uncommon, among both non-Orthodox and Orthodox in the west (and increasingly even among Orthodox in traditionally Orthodox countries), for the ancient tradition of spiritual eldership to be either unknown or misunderstood. The central role, however, that the relation of elder to spiritual child has played in the life of the Church throughout Christian history attests to its legitimacy. Similarly, the existence of living links to this Christian tradition, inherited from one generation to the next, even to the present day, attests to its vitality.

Although an academic exposition of the historical roots of eldership falls outside the scope of the present work, we do feel it necessary to look at these roots in general outline so as to place the present work in its proper context.[1] This outline necessarily begins with the New Testament witness, which may then be traced historically to the present day, and to the elders in this book.

Spiritual eldership, preserved by the Holy Spirit from apostolic

[1] For a more complete exposition, the reader may consult Bishop Kallistos (Ware's) "The Spiritual Father in Saint John Climacus and Saint Symeon the New Theologian," the Foreword of Irenee Hausherr's *Spiritual Direction in the Early Christian East.* Kalamazoo, MI: Cistercian Publications, 1990, vii-xxxiii. Also, by the same author, "The Spiritual Guide in Orthodox Christianity," published in *The Inner Kingdom: Volume One of the Collected Works.* Crestwood, NY: St. Vladimir's Press, 2000, 127-151.

times, descends to us in much the same way as does apostolic succession (understood as the historical succession of bishops from apostolic times until the present). As Bishop Kallistos (Ware) explains:

> Alongside this [apostolic succession], largely hidden, existing on a 'charismatic' rather than an official level, there is secondly the apostolic succession of the spiritual fathers and mothers in each generation of the Church—the succession of the saints, stretching from the apostolic age to our own day, which Saint Symeon the New Theologian termed the "golden chain."...Both types of succession are essential for the true functioning of the Body of Christ, and it is through their interaction that the life of the Church on earth is accomplished.[2]

The foundation on which the spiritual tradition of eldership is based is found in Holy Scripture. In particular, Christ's Incarnation, Death, and Resurrection reveal His *kenotic* [3] Fatherly love for His children and for the world. This love has as its goal the ontological rebirth of man from within, not the ethical improvement of man (although this is an inevitable fruit of true spiritual rebirth) from without.[4] Faithfully following Christ's example, St. Paul gives us a clear picture of what the relationship of elder to spiritual child means in practical terms. His relationship to the churches he founded is not simply the relationship of teacher to disciple: "For though ye have ten thousand instructors

[2] "The Spiritual Father in Saint John Climacus and Saint Symeon the New Theologian," Ibid, vii.

[3] *Kenosis/kenotic*: A Greek word meaning self-emptying.

[4] We are not aware of a sufficient study in English that addresses the crucial difference between an ethical and an ontological understanding of Christianity, although it is touched upon in Eugene Rose's (the future Fr. Seraphim (Rose)) "Christian Love," in *Heavenly Realm*. Platina, CA: St. Herman Brotherhood, 1984, 27-29.

in Christ, yet have ye not many fathers: for in Christ Jesus I have begotten you through the gospel. Wherefore I beseech you, be ye followers of me" (I Corinthians 4:15-16). St. Paul's birth imagery is significant here, as the relationship of mother to child is transposed onto the spiritual plane. His words also indicate the completely free nature of this relationship: full of love for his spiritual children, and selflessly interested in their spiritual well-being, he beseeches them to follow his example.[5] In his letter to the Galatians, St. Paul uses similar imagery, "My little children, of whom I travail in birth again until Christ be formed in you" (Galatians 4:19). As is clear from these passages, St. Paul does not see his role as that of a simple teacher, who teaches people and then leaves them to their own devices, nor as a psychologist, who tries to provide psychological answers to spiritual questions. He accepts responsibility for his children, identifying himself with them: "Who is weak, and I am not weak? Who is offended, and my heart is not ablaze with indignation?" (2 Corinthians 11:29). Bishop Kallistos develops this point a bit further: "He helps his children in Christ precisely because he is willing to share himself with them, identifying his own life with theirs. All this is true also of the spiritual father at a later date. Dostoevsky's description of the starets may be applied exactly to the ministry of Saint Paul: like the elder, the apostle is one who 'takes your soul and your will into his soul and will.'"[6] It is significant here, furthermore, that the elder does not assert his own will upon the spiritual child. On the contrary, he accepts the spiritual child as he is, receiving the child's soul into his own soul. This most basic aspect of this spiritual relationship points

---

[5] As St. John Chrysostom assures us, "He [St. Paul] is not setting forth his dignity herein, but the excess of his love." [Homily 13, PG 61:111 (col. 109). In English: *Homilies*. Found in *The Nicene and Post-Nicene Fathers of the Christian Church*. First Series. Philip Schaff, ed. Grand Rapids, MI: Wm. B. Eerdmans, Vol. XII, 1969].

[6] ibid., viii-ix.

to one of the reasons that this ancient ministry is so uncommon, especially today.

The ability of the elder to "take your soul and your will into his soul and will" is a fruit of his own willingness to empty himself (according to the *kenosis* Christ teaches by His example on the Cross) and thus make room for others. This self-emptying is not superficial, but ontological, such that there is a real identification of the elder with the life of his spiritual child.[7] Such a total commitment to other people requires complete self-sacrifice, as well as advancement along the spiritual path. Without experiential knowledge of the spiritual path the elder is practically unable to help others.[8]

When experiential knowledge of the spiritual path is absent, humanity seeks other ways to deal with its spiritual illnesses. The solution of modern man has been to provide materialistic answers to spiritual problems. Psychology, modern medicine, and so on attempt to heal man; however, detached as they are from genuine Orthodox Christian spiritual life, their attempts to answer the very deep existential problems of contemporary man remain hopelessly ineffectual. The Holy Spirit, abiding in the Church and guiding Her into all truth (John 16:13) since Pentecost, has taught the Church the ways of spiritual healing,

[7] According to St. Silouan the Athonite, this is the deeper meaning of Christ's second commandment, "Thou shalt love...thy neighbor as thyself" (Luke 10: 27). St. Silouan taught that this love is not quantitative (i.e. "as *much* as you love yourself,") but qualitative (i.e. "in the *same way* as you love yourself,") thus emphasizing that the perfection of love for others is realized in one's complete identification with them. Dr. Mantzaridis, in the foreword that follows, develops precisely this point. It is only in people's identification with Christ and with their neighbors that the true union of humanity is possible.

[8] St. John Climacus explains this necessary aspect of the elder: "A genuine teacher is he who has received from God the tablet of spiritual knowledge, inscribed by His Divine finger, that is, by the in-working of illumination, and who has no need of other books." (Ad Pastorem. PG 88: 1165B. In English: Archimandrite Lazarus Moore, *The Ladder of Divine Ascent*. Brookline, MA: Holy Transfiguration Monastery, 1991, 231).

establishing Her as a "spiritual hospital." The elder acts both as this hospital's finest surgeon as well as its chief medical school instructor.[9]

The Wisdom of the Gospel: Key to the Lives and Counsels

Perhaps the most important interpretive key for approaching the lives and counsels presented herein is the realization that they may only be understood according to their own logic, which is not the logic of this world. This logic, of course, is none other than the wisdom of Christ's life and Gospel teaching. For contemporary man, however, Christ's wisdom is truly difficult to grasp. It is a "hard" saying, and so the lives and teachings of those who have followed, experientially and existentially, the narrow path of Christ will similarly seem difficult to grasp and a "hard" saying. Early on St. Paul understood this opposition between the wisdom of the world and the wisdom of Christ:

> For it is written, I will destroy the wisdom of the wise, and will bring to nothing the understanding of the prudent. Where is the wise? Where is the scribe? Where is the disputer of this world? Hath not God made foolish the wisdom of this world? For after that in the wisdom of God the world by wisdom knew not God, it pleased God by the foolishness of preaching to save them that believe. For the Jews require a sign, and the Greeks seek after wisdom: But we preach Christ crucified, unto the Jews a stumbling block, and unto the Greeks foolishness; but unto them which are called, both Jews and

---

[9] It should be noted that this charismatic ministry is not at odds with the ministry of the priest-confessor. Both have as their goal the reconciliation of man with God. Although the priest-confessor's ministry of guidance may be hindered by the absence of experiential knowledge of the ways of spiritual growth and healing, he still bears the responsibility and blessing to hear confession, impart the forgiveness of sins, and to reconcile man to God. For more on the Orthodox understanding of the Church as spiritual hospital, see Metropolitan Hierotheos (Vlachos's) *Orthodox Psychotherapy*. Levadia, Greece: Birth of the Theotokos Monastery, 1994.

Greeks, Christ the power of God, and the wisdom of God. Because the foolishness of God is wiser than men; and the weakness of God is stronger than men (1 Corinthians 1: 19-25).

Accepting Christ's message (and the incarnation of this message in the lives of the elders gathered here) is particularly difficult for contemporary people, even faithful Christians, for many of us live most of our lives according to the wisdom of this world and not according to the "foolishness" of the Cross. When one understands that a chasm lies between worldly wisdom and the wisdom of the Gospel, it makes the comprehension of the following lives more realizable. When this shift in vision is accomplished, it reveals one's poverty of faith, as well as the distance between where one is and the absolute demands of the Gospel commandments.

For the person who is seeking God, this realization of the absolute difference between the wisdom of this world and the wisdom of the Gospel begets repentance. It is significant that the Greek word for repentance, *metanoia*, literally means a "change of mind." This change of mind is a prerequisite for the comprehension of the Gospel, so it is not surprising that St. John the Baptist began his public ministry with the injunction, "Repent ye: for the kingdom of heaven is at hand." (Matthew 3: 2). Likewise, Christ began His ministry with the same message: "From that time Jesus began to preach, and to say, Repent: for the kingdom of heaven is at hand" (Matthew 4:17). That the lives and counsels of the elders contained in this book force the reader to shift to the wisdom of the Gospel testifies to their spiritual ministry as prophets, a ministry that monasticism has always fulfilled.[10]

Given the context of the wisdom of the Gospel, the aspects of these lives that surpass human understanding should not shock

[10] "And God hath set some in the church, first apostles, secondarily prophets,

or scandalize. Christ told His disciples that, "He that believeth on me, the works that I do shall he do also; and greater works than these shall he do" (John 14:12). The Church in Her wisdom and strength has preserved the witness of those who, in the two thousand years since Christ's coming, have followed faithfully in His steps. The lives of the Saints and the writings of ancient and contemporary Fathers of the Church[11]give unquestionable witness to the riches of God's mercy and the experience of the action of the Holy Spirit. The lives and sayings contained herein are contemporary witnesses to the truth that the Holy Spirit has not ceased to fashion precious vessels in the image and likeness of the Holy Trinity.

The present book has been compiled to witness to this truth, and this witness is the most precious aspect of these lives (rather than their miraculous aspect, impressive though this may be). One may legitimately object, after reading the lives, that the culture in which these men were raised is significantly different from that in which we live. The testimony we have from the Fathers of the Church, however, is that the place in which we live is less significant than the way in which we live. They tell us, furthermore, that there are no circumstances that could prevent us from keeping Christ's commandments, from following the way Christ has shown us.[12] This is also the witness of the Scrip-

thirdly teachers..." (1 Corinthians 12:28). This prophetic ministry was central to both the Old and New Testaments. The roots of monasticism lie in this ancient ministry, which is not so much concerned with telling the future (although this aspect of the prophetic ministry continues up to the present day), as calling the world to a change of heart, to repentance, so that the world might more readily accept the Gospel message.

[11] Fathers of the Church: This term is used in the Orthodox Church to refer to Saints of all times whose teaching has been accepted by the Church as an authentic expression of Her life and faith. Roman Catholics tend to define this term more narrowly, limiting the Fathers to those Saints of the Church who lived during the "golden age" of theology, in the first millennium of Christianity, whose writings played a significant role in the development of the dogmatic expression of the faith.

[12] St. Symeon the New Theologian goes so far as to say that to believe otherwise

tures, wherein we understand that the Scriptural injunctions are not dependent on time or place, but are always pertinent and binding on man.[13]

To many, the absolute character of Christ's commandments may seem a heavy burden. Again, however, the wisdom of the Gospel surprises us, as Christ says, "Come unto me, all ye that labour and are heavy laden, and I will give you rest. Take my yoke upon you, and learn of me; for I am meek and lowly in heart: and ye shall find rest unto your souls. For my yoke is easy, and my burden is light" (Matthew 11:28-30).[14]

Perhaps more than anything else the lives of the Saints (and of the elders in this book) provide an "interpretation" of Christ's Gospel, "written not with ink, but with the Spirit of the living God; not in tables of stone, but in fleshly tables of the heart" (2 Corinthians 3:3). That which is of greatest importance in these lives are not so much the details of each life, but rather the spirit that breathes in them, which shaped them into precious vessels of the Holy Spirit. These lives bear witness to the transformation of man that is possible, when the Christian gives himself wholly over to the will of God. As Elder Sophrony of Essex has written, it is not arbitrary asceticism or the possession of supernatural gifts that constitute genuine Christian spiritual life, but rather obedience to the will of God. Each person has his own capabilities and his own path to tread; the keeping of Christ's commandments, however, remains a constant. Fr. Sophrony also repeatedly insists, following the teaching of his elder, St. Silouan the Athonite,

is heresy: "But the men of whom I speak and whom I call heretics are those who say that there is no one in our times and in our midst who is able to keep the Gospel commandments and become like the holy Fathers." *The Discourses.* (Trans. C.J. deCatanzaro), Mahwah, NJ: Paulist Press, 1980, 312. See also, Archimandrite Sophrony (Sakharov), *St. Silouan the Athonite.* Essex, England: Stavropegic Monastery of St. John the Baptist, 1991, 242-243.

[13] See Matthew 5:18 and 24:35, Mark 13:31, and Luke 21:33, among others.

[14] "But if virtue seems a difficult thing consider that vice is more difficult. . . . Sin, too, has labor, and a burden that is heavy and hard to bear...." (Homily 38, St. John Chrysostom, *ibid*).

that the truth or falsity of one's path may be measured, not by one's asceticism or spiritual gifts, but by love for one's enemies, by which St. Silouan did not mean a "scornful pity; for him the *compassion* of a loving heart was an indication of the trueness of the Divine path."[15] In another place Fr. Sophrony develops this point more fully:

> There are known instances when Blessed Staretz Silouan in prayer beheld something remote as though it were happening close by; when he saw into someone's future, or when profound secrets of the human soul were revealed to him. There are many people still alive who can bear witness to this in their own case, but he himself never aspired to it and never accorded much significance to it. His soul was totally engulfed in compassion for the world. He concentrated himself utterly on prayer for the world, and in his spiritual life prized this love above all else.[16]

Fr. Sophrony's words reveal to us a mystery of the ways of Christian monasticism and eldership: according to the wisdom of this world, the monastic elder's departure from the world seems like an escape from humanity. In reality, according to the wisdom of the gospel, separation from the world enables those who love God to love the world more than those who live in the world do. It is this paradox that the monastic elder lives, and an explication of which Dr. Georgios Mantzaridis provides in his foreword.[17]

---

[15] Archimandrite Sophrony (Sakharov), *St. Silouan the Athonite*, 228.

[16] Ibid., 130.

[17] One final note: concerning the application of the spiritual principles found in this book to one's own life, as with all aspects of the spiritual life, spiritual guidance is a necessary prerequisite for spiritual growth.

Elder Joseph the Hesychast as a young monk

UNIVERSALITY AND MONASTICISM[1]

Professor Georgios Mantzaridis, Ph.D.

The tendency towards unity and universality is in opposition to the tendency towards separation and isolation. Many place the movement toward monasticism, which may be observed today, in this second category. In fact, particularly in the Orthodox world, this movement appears particularly strong. So, what relation can monasticism have to universality? Perhaps it is antithetical to it? Perhaps it is in conflict with it? Or, perhaps monasticism also has universality as its goal, and can give an answer to the failed attempt to live this universality on the level of worldly life?

The greatest ascetics of the Church, such as Anthony the Great, the holy monastic Saints Euthymios, Ephraim the Syrian, Neilos the Ascetic, Silouan the Athonite, and so on, are characterized as "Universal Fathers."[2] This characterization does not simply suggest the scope of their teachings, but also the characteristic

---

[1] This foreword first appeared in Dr. Mantzaridis's book Παγκοσμιοποίηση και παγκοσμιότητα, Χίμαιρα και Αλήθεια [Globalization and Universality: Chimera and Truth.] Thessalonica, Greece: P. Pounaras Publications, 2001. [Tr.]

[2] See, for example, Stichera Prosomoia of Vespers of Cheese-fare Friday. Kontakion of St. Ephraim of Syria, Matins of January 28. Kontakion of St. Silouan the Athonite, Matins of September 24.

of their person.[3] More precisely, it conveys that characteristic of their person that is expressed in the scope of their teaching and of their example. The true monk is a universal man, and the goal of monasticism is the perfection of man, which coincides with his showing forth as universal.

This truth, however, seems strange. Universality is generally connected to extroversion, and to social relations, while monasticism is connected to contemplation and introversion. Universality is usually sought after through various encounters and affiliations, while monasticism is cultivated through the flight from the world and isolation. Is that, however, the way things actually are? Is universality the fruit of extroversion and social relations? Can it be realized through compromised encounters and affiliations? But also, on the other hand, is universality in conflict with contemplation and introversion? Is it hindered by the flight from the world and by the search for stillness?

Humanity does not exist outside of man; it does not move in an ethereal realm. Humanity is found within man, in everyone. The first man had within himself, in potential, the whole human race.[4] Every person, in fact, contains in his nature all humanity. Man, however, moved by selfishness, which is the mother of every

[3] Person: The "person" (or "hypostasis," which is here used with the same meaning) according to St. John of Damascus, "is one who by reason of his own operations and properties exhibits to us an appearance which is distinct and set off from those of the same nature as he...." (*Writings.* [*The Fount of Knowledge*], ch. 43. Translation: Frederic H. Chase, JR., *The Fathers of the Church*, vol. 37, Washington D.C.: Catholic University Press, 1999, 67). The term combines two main ideas—the common shared nature and the distinct person/hypostasis, which, while being connected to all others of the same nature, at the same time does not lose its personal qualities. Person/Hypostasis is here differentiated from "individual," which does not include the concept of a shared nature, but rather emphasizes the distinctions among beings. [Tr.]

[4] "Even though Adam was created as one man, in him there existed, in potential [οι λόγοι], the succession of all generations." St. Athanasios the

human passion, is confined to his individualism, and is unable to see the unity of the human race. He is unable to accept and to live the life of all humanity within himself, so as to become a true human person. Universality as a qualitative category is not realized through the agreement of people, not even of all the people in the world, but through their inclusion and union[5] in every particular human person. Universality does not abolish, but rather reveals the person. More precisely, universality is the characteristic of the true person, of the true hypostasis.

The fall into sin destroyed man internally and divided the human race into egocentric individuals. Man's distancing from the source of life, God, killed him and estranged him from his neighbor and from the world. Man's subjection to the law of decay and death left him egocentric and selfish. In this way, the unity of humanity was undermined at its base and division became the rule.

The unity or division of humanity is also the unity or division of every person. Furthermore, the unity or division of every person is reflected in all of humanity. Every person, with the way he lives and acts, with the way he exists and expresses himself in the world, unifies or divides all humanity. The unity of man or of humanity does not exist without a hypostasis, but is incarnated [υποστασιάζεται] in human persons. Division is that which is without hypostasis (that is, which lacks the personal dimension) and this destroys hypostasis.

Divided people are not able to form a unified world. The division of the world externalizes the internal division of man. The center of universal division is found in the heart of man, in the inner man. This division, which is created in the heart, surpasses every external division. This is the reason that the

Great, *Κατά Αρειανών* 2.48, PG 26, 249C.

[5] The Greek word Dr. Mantzaridis uses is *sing-horesi* (συγχώρηση), which, beyond the idea of "union," includes the idea of making space in one's life for the other, so that people can share the same space together. [Tr.]

foundation of the unification of the world, the foundation of true universality, is found in the heart of man.

The monk cultivates his internal unity by bringing his mind, which is dispersed in the environment, into his heart; into the spiritual center of his being. Love for God, which is the foundation of Christian life, is born in the heart of man through faith. When the heart of man burns with love for God, it assimilates the mind and in this way man is unified, is healed.[6]

In order for the monk to realize this healing, he separates from the world and focuses on himself. This action seems egotistic and divisive as regards his relation to the world. However, the love for self, good selfishness, dictates that the monk make this movement of contraction and of separation, if he is to find his internal unity. When, however, he finds his internal unity, he re-affirms his unity with all humanity. This is then followed by the other movement: the movement toward expansion and the taking in of the whole world, the movement toward true universality. The movement of contraction is the human action; it is man's synergy. The movement of expansion is the divine synergy; it is the energy of God, which is revealed within man, and which works along with man.

True universality is established in the universal man. Universal humanity is a result of the appearance of universal people. Without these people there may be universal phenomena, but there cannot be substantive universality. The establishment of universality is attempted in our day, through people's use of the negative elements of modernism. How can they possibly succeed, when internal division rules man, when human nature itself is continually divided and leaves people increasingly egocentric and selfish?

[6] See Archimandrite Sophrony (Sakharov), Οψόμεθα τον Θεόν καθώς εστί Essex, England: Stavropegic Monastery of St. John the Baptist, 1996, 272-273 (in English: *We Shall See Him As He Is*. Essex, England: Stavropegic

The answer cannot be based on divided humanity, but rather must be sought within the perspective of a dynamic new human *becoming* [γίγνεσθαι].[7] Nor can this new human *becoming* unify humanity's being, if it is not realized within human nature, freeing it from decay and division. This is exactly what happens with Christ and His Church.

Man, who was created "in the image and according to the likeness" of God, acts as a mirror (ἔσοπτρον) that resonates or reflects God Himself. The person who reaches perfection becomes god in all things, "without the identification of nature."[8] This, however, becomes possible only when the mirror's (ἔσοπτρον) surface is clean. Whatever is on this surface, not only a black mark or dust, but also valuable gems or pearls, prohibits the proper reflection, or, at best, creates misshapen refractions.

The monk's goal is his release from every worldly obstacle: his liberation from passions, belongings, and his own will. It is complete *kenosis* and it is to this end that the three monastic virtues: virginity, poverty, and obedience, are directed. Obedience in particular, which is the chief monastic virtue, aims at perfect *kenosis* and humility. In fact, no virtue is an end in itself, but is the means for the cultivation of humility; that is, man's complete release from everything that separates him from God and neighbor.

"The monk is he who separates himself from all things and who is united to all things." Also, "the monk is he who is with everyone such that in each person he continuously finds himself."[9] The

Monastery of St. John the Baptist, 1988).

[7] We have translated το γίγνεσθαι as *becoming*, which will be italicized in the text. The word denotes development, transformation, creation. [Tr.]

[8] Maximos the Confessor, *Ἐπιστολή* 1. PG 91, 376 B.

[9] Evagrios Ponticus, *Περί Εὐχῆς* 124-125, PG 79, 1193C.

monk separates himself from everything, so as to be united to everything. He is with everyone, for he sees in the other his true self, for the other is his true self. "So we, being many, are one body in Christ, and every one members one of another" (Romans 12:5). His ultimate goal is acceptance, not rejection; it is union, not division. In order for the union with all to be realized, separation from all must come first; only then does man unite with God. When he unites with God, he is united with everyone, and with everything. If the reality of division is not abandoned, the sought-after union cannot be realized. If individualism is not destroyed, the universal cannot appear.

St. Maximos the Confessor emphasizes five great divisions in the nature of beings. The first division is that which exists between uncreated and created nature. The second is the division of creation into noetic and sensible. The third is the division of sensible nature into heaven and earth. The fourth is the division of the earth into universe and paradise. The fifth, finally, is the division that divides man into male and female.[10] Man, who was created last, "exactly like a workshop which unifies everything," received the possibility of unifying these five divisions, starting with the human division and progressively reaching the division between created and uncreated.

Man, however, not only failed to progress in the lifting of the divisions, but did the opposite. He moved in a way that was "contrary to nature, willingly, in a foolish manner," and heightened the divisions, in danger of being submerged in non-being.[11] It is for this reason that God became man, so as to save man, and to unify all divisions. In this way Christ began His unifying work with His birth from the Virgin, which lifted the division between male and female. With His renewal in the world, with His death and resurrection, He achieved the unification of the universe and paradise. Then, with His ascension, He united heaven and earth, and with His passage

[10] See Maximos the Confessor, Περί αποριών. PG 91, 1304D-1305B.

[11] Ibid., PG 91, 1305A, etc.

Precious Vessels

as man through all the sensible and noetic realms, He united all creation. Finally, with His appearance as man before God the Father, He united everything.

The appearance of Christ in the world and in history opens up a new perspective. Man, in the body of Christ, the Church, is called to surpass his broken nature and to proceed in the dynamic new human *becoming*, which Christ revealed. This new *becoming* demands the mortification of the old man. It is for this reason that, from the beginning of the Christian life, the Cross is thrust to the foreground.[12] Lifting up the Cross and walking with Christ are not undertaken for man's undoing, but for the honoring of man. They are aimed at man's perfection as a person.

The monk does nothing more than attempt to faithfully respond to this invitation of Christ. Virginity does not have a negative meaning, but a positive one. Monasticism is not grounded upon the rejection of the flesh and of the life of the flesh. The Canons of the Church condemn those who take refuge in the monastic life out of contempt for marriage or disdain for fleshly union.[13] The goal of the monk's virginity is the lifting of the division of human nature into male and female. With his mortification of the things of the world, which is at the same time resurrection and life on the level of spiritual life, he lives the unity of the universe and paradise. With his participation in the way of life of the children of the kingdom of heaven he lives the unity of heaven and earth; while, with the living of the angelic life while still in the body, he lives the unity of the sensible and noetic. Finally, with his appearance before God in his pure and unceasing prayer, he lives the unity of everything.

The reality of division is preserved through individualism.

---

[12] "If any man will come after me, let him deny himself, and take up his cross, and follow me" (Matthew 16:24).

[13] See Apostolic Canons 5 and 51, as well as Canons 1, 9 and 14 of the Synod of Gangra. Cf. Archimandrite Sophrony (Sakharov), Άσκηση και Θεωρία, Essex, England, 1996, 64.

To the extent that man has himself as center and views things according to the criteria of his own interests, he distinguishes and separates himself from others. Even when he is transferred from his individual *me* to the *we* of the family or of some wider racial, social, or ethnic group, he continues to move in the bounds of division. He is not perfected as a person, nor does he become universal. The passage from individual to collective egotism widens man's conscience to a certain extent, but does not substantially alter his path or his mentality. It does not establish him as a person of love.

The monk abandons family and the wider society that surrounds him, so as to be included in the universal family of God; so as to become a person of love, as God himself is love. This passage is neither easy nor painless. For this reason, moreover, it is not always realizable. The passage from individual and collective egotism to the catholicity and universality of love establishes man as a true person. And this is realized in the perspective of the new human *becoming*, which Christ revealed. It is precisely with this perspective that the Apostle Paul preaches, "There is neither Jew nor Greek, there is neither bond nor free, there is neither male nor female: for ye are all one in Christ Jesus" (Galatians 3:28).

This is the goal of the monk. This must also, however, be the goal of every Christian, for the monk aspires to nothing more than that to which every Christian must aspire, who desires to attain perfection. St. Maximos the Confessor explains that when man is perfected in love and impassibility (απάθεια), "He does not see a difference between one of his own and a foreigner...or between a believer and a non-believer, or between a slave and a freeman, or even between male and female; but having become greater than the tyranny of the passions, and aiming at the realization of one nature, he views everyone without distinction, and behaves the same towards everyone."[14] In particular, the surpassing of the difference of the sexes in monasticism is suggested by the raiment that is given to both monks and nuns during the tonsure, as well as by the identical form of life that they undertake to follow. Differences are not leveled here, but are surpassed in the perspective of the perfecting of persons.

The passage from egocentrism and egotism to catholicity and universality follows a path that is the reverse of that of the fall. That is to say, while the fall and division of man began and continue through disobedience, the withdrawal of love, and the denial of personal responsibility for the evil that appears in the world, the rectification of the fall, and the path toward universality and catholicity began and continue through obedience, the living of love, and the personal acceptance of responsibility for evil and its confrontation. Man does not confront the evil that appears in the world as something foreign and unrelated to himself, but he sees it as personal evil. He sees it in this way, because all humanity is, for him, a universal being, which is contained in his hypostatic being, without the reduction of the existence of all other hypostases.[15]

The opening towards universality begins with a fundamental change. It begins with the purification and return of man to himself and to God. As man returns to himself, purified from the passions, he sees God Who is sketched within him. Seeing God, he sees his true self. He sees the true human, who is a horizon of revelation of all of the God-man's being. "Behold, the heavens are within you, if you are pure; and within you, you will see the angels and their light, and their master with them and within them."[16]

This change does not take place on the psychological or social level, but has an ontological character. It is a change that is realized through man's voluntary crucifixion and his incorporation into

[14] Maximos the Confessor, *Κεφάλαια Περί Αγάπης.* 2, 30, PG 90, 993B.

[15] See Archimandrite Sophrony (Sakharov), *Ο Άγιος Σιλουανός ο Αθωνίτης.* Essex, England: Stavropegic Monastery of St. John the Baptist, 1999, 163 (in English: *St. Silouan the Athonite*).

[16] Isaac the Syrian, *Λόγος* 43. I. Spetsieri Publications, 176.

the perspective of the new creation. The psychological and social levels are neither useless, nor inconsequential. On the contrary, they are useful and even necessary, so that man is able to understand the ontological change in his life. For this reason, moreover, there is the institution of monasticism, which transforms the social and psychological framework by ontological renewal. Man denies himself so that the new man may be born within him. He mortifies his being so as to regain it with the new *becoming*. He abandons the divisions of the past, so as to live the future unity of all things.

The foundation and indication of this change is Christ. He is the new Adam, Who from limitless love took upon Himself the sin of all the world and died so as to abolish it. Taking on Himself the sin of the world, He bore all of humanity, "For all have sinned" (Romans 3:23). Man's true approach to life is not realized on the level of holiness, but on the level of sinfulness. It doesn't happen in paradise, but in hell. When man puts his mind in hell, nothing separates him from anyone. As Christ did, so does the Christian truly approach his neighbor, when he shoulders the responsibility for his sin. Whoever shoulders this responsibility for his neighbor, truly and completely, sees the salvific death of Christ as a sacrifice that took place for his own personal sin. In this way the Apostle Paul sees the sacrifice of Christ as a sacrifice that was made personally for himself.[17] This understanding of things does not reveal conceit, but perfect humility, for here the Apostle shares the universal responsibility that led Christ to the Cross.

In the same vein is the seeking of personal mercy with the phrase, "Have mercy on me," in place of, "Have mercy on us." When the monk says, "Lord Jesus Christ, have mercy on me," he does not egotistically separate himself from others; but, on

---

[17] "The life which I now live in the flesh I live by the faith of the Son of God, who loved me, and gave himself for me" (Galatians 2:20).

the contrary, he bears within himself all others, broadening his love without bounds, and shouldering their responsibility. Elder Porphyrios would say, "Don't you know that you and I are one?...In this feeling of our unity with the other is hidden the mystery of the spiritual life in Christ."[18] For this reason he would encourage his spiritual children, when they would pray for someone, to take the person's place and to say again, "Lord Jesus Christ, have mercy on me."

The perfect monk voluntarily shoulders the universal responsibility for the evil that exists in the world. In this way he also sees the salvation that is offered by Christ as his own personal salvation. Placing himself beneath all people and considering himself the first among sinners, he encounters Christ's gift as a personal gift. He becomes universal on the level of universal sin and accepts the universal reconciliation with the new life that Christ offers the sinful person. He becomes a participant in the condition of Christ. Just as Christ bears within Himself all humanity, so the monk is thus widened and embraces all the world. He becomes universal, "in the image of the universality of Christ Himself,"[19] and realizes the pre-eternal goal of His creation, to be, "according to the likeness" of God. When St. Silouan saw the Living Christ, he began to pray for the whole world, as for himself.[20] He became a partaker of the condition of Christ and acquired a universal consciousness.

The universality that the Church professes and encourages is based on the person and is realized with his expansion and

[18] See *Κοντά Στο Γέροντα Πορφύριο*, Athens, Greece 1995, 51 (in English: Constantine Yiannitsiotis, *With Elder Porphyrios: A Spiritual Child Remembers*. Athens, Greece: Holy Convent of the Transfiguration of the Savior, 2001).

[19] Archimandrite Sophrony (Sakharov), *Περί Προσευχής*. Essex, England: Stavropegic Monastery of St. John the Baptist, 116-117 (in English: *On Prayer*. Essex, England: Stavropegic Monastery of St. John the Baptist, 1996).

[20] Archimandrite Sophrony (Sakharov), *Ο Άγιος Σιλουανός ο Αθωνίτης*,

showing forth in a place of union[21]of the whole world, in a universal hypostasis. It is the universality of freedom. On the contrary, the globalization that is promoted in our days is based on the leveling of unique characteristics and is realized with the quantification and the destruction of persons. It is the globalization of bondage.

417 (in English: *St. Silouan the Athonite*).

[21] In Greek, συγχώρηση (see footnote above regarding this word). [Tr.]

Elder Philotheos of Paros

The holy and God-bearing Fathers wrote about great spiritual gifts not so that anyone might strive indiscriminately to receive them, but so that those who do not have them, hearing about such exalted gifts and revelations which were received by those who were worthy, might acknowledge their own profound infirmity and great insufficiency, and might involuntarily be inclined to humility, which is more necessary for those seeking salvation than all other works and virtues.

- Saint Makarios of Optina

Elder Amphilochios of Patmos

1

ELDER AMPHILOCHIOS

T he blessed Elder Amphilochios (Makris) was born December 13, 1889, on the holy island of Patmos, where St. John the Evangelist received and wrote the final book of the New Testament, *Revelation*. His pious parents Emmanuel and Irene gave him the name Athanasios in baptism. As with many holy elders and Saints of the Church, Athanasios was born into a large family of simple country folk. Family stories tell of the piety of Athanasios's paternal grandparents and the ways in which they were visited by divine grace. Little Athanasios seemed to have an innate sense of the Church's *phronyma*[1] and thus refused his mother's milk on Wednesdays and Fridays.[2] At the tender

---

[1] *Phronyma*: A Greek word denoting the proper spirit, understanding, etc. of those in the Orthodox Church. Proper *phronyma* is a natural result of a life lived truly in the Church.

[2] Orthodox faithful follow the fasting prescribed by the Church. On Wednesdays and Fridays throughout the year (with few exceptions), as well as during other periods, the faithful fast from meat, dairy products, oil, and wine. Such manifestations of piety in infants are not uncommon in the lives of the Saints. In addition to the testimony of the Saints and of contemporary elders, there are also numerous accounts in Holy Scripture that testify to the spiritual perception of infants. Such divine manifestations help explain how the Orthodox Church developed its understanding of man, the fall, and ancestral sin, which differs considerably from the theological position of

age of five, he managed to convince his godmother, who had just gotten engaged, to call off the engagement and to live out the rest of her days in virginity. Athanasios preserved himself from the temptations of the world and, by the age of seventeen, decided with certainty to enter a monastery. His parents were happy to give their blessing, and so the young Athanasios became a novice at the Monastery of St. John the Theologian, Patmos, in March of 1906. He quickly became beloved of the aging brotherhood, and, progressing in virtue and asceticism, he was made a *rasaphore*[3] monk in August of the same year, at which time he was given the name Amphilochios.

The young monk Amphilochios was strict with himself. Aware of his various shortcomings, he devised ways of combating his sinful tendencies, so as to advance spiritually. He was especially strict in his eating and would eat no more than ten mouthfuls of food at each meal, while on fast days he would eat only seven or eight olives. After seven years in the monastery, he had progressed sufficiently so as to be deemed ready to take the *Great Schema*[4] in March of 1913. Amphilochios's spiritual father, Elder

Western Christianity. For more discussion regarding this question, see the glossary entry, *Ancestral Sin*.

[3] *Rasaphore*: A Greek word meaning "cassock-wearing." It is the second stage in monasticism, after the noviate, during which time the candidate for monasticism is given the blessing to wear the black monastic garb.

[4] *Great Schema*: The final stage of monastic profession, wherein the monastic makes complete promises. It was revealed to a Russian monk, a disciple of St. Philaret of Moscow, that the chief characteristic of the monk of the *Great Schema* is prayer for the whole world. It should be noted that there are various monastic practices as regards the chronology of the tonsures to *Rasaphore*, *Small Schema*, and *Great Schema*. These three stages of monastic life correspond to the three renunciations addressed in St. John Klimakos's *Ladder of Divine Ascent*. For a more detailed account of the stages of monastic growth, see Archimandrite Sophrony (Sakharov's) "Principles in

Antoniadis, performed the tonsure.[5] It is not insignificant that Fr. Antoniadis was a spiritual son of the fathers of the *Kolly-vades* Movement,[6] which had brought spiritual rejuvenation to the Greeks, so afflicted under the Turkish yoke. This helps explain the missionary and ascetic zeal of Elder Amphilochios.

Fr. Amphilochios was completely dedicated to his monastic profession. He did, however, retain the hope of eventually making pilgrimages for spiritual edification. This was realized in 1911 when the abbot of the monastery decided to send the young Amphilochios to Mt. Athos,[7] so as to learn woodcarving. It was a soul-profiting visit that he remembered fondly until the end of his days.

A few years later, in May of 1913, the abbot, recognizing Amphilochios's virtue and progress, secured the agreement of the brethren of the monastery to have him ordained to the diaconate. They sent him to the island of Kos to be ordained by the bishop there. Amphilochios's concern, however, for his inadequacy and unworthiness led him to change his course. To

Orthodox Asceticism," in *Orthodox Ethos, Studies in Orthodoxy*. Oxford UK; Holywell Press, 1964, 259-286.

[5] Tonsure: The action of making a person a monk.

[6] The *Kollyvades* Movement of the early nineteenth century was led by Sts. Nikodemos of the Holy Mountain, Makarios Notaras, and Athanasios of Paros, and addressed various pastoral irregularities that had entered ecclesiastical life during the Turkish occupation. The two issues that most concerned them were the restoration of frequent communion and the preservation of the resurrectional character of Sunday, in particular, the cessation of memorial services on Sunday. Their goal was the proper spiritual education of the people so that they might live a fuller life as conscientious Christians.

[7] Mt. Athos, also known as the Holy Mountain, is a monastic republic located on a peninsula in northern Greece. For over a thousand years Mt. Athos has been the most important center of Orthodox monasticism. The Holy Mountain plays a prominent role in many of the lives in this book, testifying

his traveling companion, one of the brethren of the monastery who was also to be ordained, he explained, "My brother, I am unworthy of such an honor. I would rather go from place to place begging alms, with a clean conscience, than unworthily take on the honor of ordination. Go on in peace, I'm going to head towards the Holy Lands."

In this way, Fr. Amphilochios's sense of unworthiness, coupled with his characteristic freedom of spirit and his fervent desire to see the Holy Places, led him to travel to Egypt and then on to the Holy Lands.[8] He was very moved by his pilgrimage and decided to ask the Patriarch of Jerusalem to receive him as one of the caretakers of the Holy Sepulchre.[9] Although the Patriarch

to its influence on the spiritual life of Greece. This said, it must be noted that the composition of Mt. Athos is oecumenical—it has monks from all over the world as well as a Bulgarian, a Russian, a Serb, and many Greek monasteries. At one time there were also Albanian, Amalfitan, Georgian, Moldavian, and Wallachian monasteries.

[8] A fervent desire to visit the places where Christ lived is a common theme in the lives of the Saints and of contemporary elders. Elder Amphilochios's "freedom of spirit" should not be confused with anarchic "freedom," as it is understood in the West. About this freedom St. Silouan explains, "People generally seek freedom in order to do what they like. But that is not freedom but the power of sin over you....True freedom means constant dwelling in God" (Archimandrite Sophrony (Sakharov), *St. Silouan the Athonite*, 65). Thus, what seems to the worldly mind to be flagrant disobedience, in the life and experiences of the Saints of the Church, proves to be beyond human ethics. This true freedom of spirit is a common theme throughout the lives of the Saints and contemporary elders. We may go to the Holy Scriptures to find an explanation for this phenomenon. As St. Paul explains, "He that is spiritual judgeth all things, yet he himself is judged of no man" (1 Corinthians 2:15).

[9] Holy Sepulchre: The church built over the tomb where Christ was buried.

was willing to receive him, the brethren of the Monastery of St. John the Theologian on Patmos insisted that he return to the monastery of his repentance.[10] On his return to Patmos, the brethren "punished" him for his disobedience by sending him to the hermitage of Apollo, to live beside the Elder Makarios. As it turned out, he was very happy there, able as he was to give himself over completely to prayer in the silence of the desert.

From early on, Elder Amphilochios had dreamed of eventually helping his countrymen, spiritually weakened after hundreds of years of Turkish oppression and foreign rule, to discover their spiritual roots and to delve deeper into the spiritual life. Already, as just a simple monk in the monastery, he managed to procure a plot of land on a rocky slope of western Patmos. He built two cells adjacent to the chapel already there and dreamed of eventually building a monastery for women. Eventually, in 1920, God brought Amphilochios his first co-worker in the mission field, Kalliope Gounaris (the future nun Evstokia).

Significant in the Elder's missionary endeavors was his ordination to the diaconate in 1919 and to the priesthood soon afterwards, due to the continued pressure of the brethren of the monastery. Though bringing him added responsibilities, his ordination also enabled him to serve the liturgy freely, to receive spiritual children, and to bring the grace of the Mysteries[11] to his mission work. Soon after his ordination he was sent to serve at the monastery's dependency[12] on the island of Kos. This was also the first period of his missionary travels during which time, in addition to his service as priest in the Monastery of St. John the

[10] That is, the monastery where he was tonsured a monk.

[11] Mysteries: Throughout the text we translate the Greek word *mysterion* as "Mystery," as it better reflects the theological meaning of the original Greek than does the word "sacrament."

[12] Dependency (also known as *metochi*): Any building owned and maintained by a monastery, which exists outside the property of the monastery. This includes churches, farmland, guesthouses for traveling monks, and so on.

Theologian, he served as a confessor throughout the islands of the Dodecanese. Much of his time and energy was spent on the island of Kalymnos, where Kalliope Gounaris was working as a teacher, and where the nucleus of a monastery for women was beginning to develop.

In 1926 the Elder was sent by his monastery to serve at the cave of the Apocalypse on Patmos.[13] During this period he spent a good deal of time with students of the Ecclesiastical Academy of Patmos. His concern was that they mature spiritually and intellectually so as to be useful servants of the Church and society. The many seeds he planted bore much fruit, including numerous elders and abbots of monasteries.

By 1935 a difficult situation had developed among the islands occupied by the Italians. The Italians had managed to influence the Church and the monasteries there by forcing a system of governance upon the Church that made it easy for them to manipulate the Church to their advantage. When the question of the new abbacy of the monastery was raised in 1935, the Oecumenical Patriarch (under whom the Dodecanese are governed ecclesiastically) insisted that this anomalous situation be rectified. The brotherhood elected Elder Amphilochios to be abbot, undermining the authority of the Italians, who wanted one of their puppets elected.

Soon after his election as abbot, the door opened for what would be the seeds of the future women's Monastery of the Annunciation, fifteen minutes by foot from the Monastery of St. John. Initially the building there was to house a training workshop for knitting and weaving. The secret reason for the establishment of the workshop was to provide an underground school where the children of Patmos could learn Greek letters, as the Italians were on the verge of prohibiting the teaching of Greek to the

[13] A hermitage has been built around the cave of the Apocalypse, where St. John the Evangelist had his visions and where he dictated the last book of

The Elder at study in his cell

children.[14] Kalliope Gounaris had by this time moved to Patmos and was to run the school along with the help of some other pious young women.

The Italians got increasingly upset by the Elder's work, and eventually removed him in 1937, exiling him to "free" Greece along with Kalliope Gounaris.[15] In place of the Elder the Italians had one of their co-workers, a monk of the monastery, elected and enthroned as abbot. The small community of the Annunciation that the Elder had managed to organize was now left without their spiritual father during the time of his exile. The Elder, who

the New Testament, *Revelation*, to his disciple.

[14] This followed the tradition of the *krypto scholeio* ("hidden school") that flourished among Greeks during the Turkish occupation. It was largely through these schools that the Greek language, culture, and identity were preserved despite the Turks' attempts to purge the Greeks of their identity.

[15] While the Dodecanese islands chain, where Patmos is located, was at the time occupied by the Italians, mainland Greece was not.

throughout his life was especially devoted to his nuns, was greatly concerned for them during this period of exile and persecution.

When the Elder arrived in Athens, he was given hospitality by the "Zoe" brotherhood in Athens. From there he traveled throughout Greece, eventually reaching Crete, where he was asked to take over the general spiritual fatherhood of the island. His exile ended in 1939, when he was received with great joy back on Patmos.

Occupation of the islands by the Italians was followed by German occupation in 1942. The Elder, exhausted from his exile, decided not to return to the abbacy of the monastery, but spent time at various dependencies of the monastery, and focused his energies on the spiritual and material establishment of the women's Monastery of the Annunciation. He carefully regulated the monastery's communal life, providing it with the foundation on which it would flourish. In addition to the monasteries on Patmos and Kalymnos, the Elder had hoped to establish women's monasteries in other parts of Greece. In time his prayers and struggles were rewarded as provision was made for monasteries on the islands of Aegina and Ikaria as well as for an ecclesiastical center and church on the island of Crete.

Elder Amphilochios had a balanced understanding of people and their needs, realizing that man is made up of both soul and body. While he placed the good of man's soul at the center of every action, he did not divide this from the other aspects of man. Thus we see that in addition to his attempts to provide centers of monastic struggle for those who sought such a life, he also sought to provide opportunities for study and for the development of each person's talents. In 1947 he was given the opportunity to help the orphans of Rhodes, whose material situation was miserable. He organized a small group of his nuns, led by Abbess Evstokia, to establish an orphanage and a unit for pregnant women.

Perhaps more than anything else Elder Amphilochios is remembered for his great love and sacrifice for the suffering people

The Elder was a spiritual father and guide to a host of spiritual strugglers, many of whom were women monastics

of God. Despite his sickness and weakness, he would receive the faithful with joy. In responding to the objections of one of the sisters, who was concerned for his health, he responded, "I am a servant of the Church and cannot rest!"

The power of his love and prayer for people is attested to in the following incident. Late one afternoon, while the Elder was in Athens, two spiritual daughters visited him. They left the house where he was staying after nightfall and he bade them good night with his blessing. He was anxious, however, for their safety, and as they left he began to pray earnestly for their safe trip home. He was especially concerned as one of the ladies had a problem with her knees and often fell. As they returned home, the infirm lady felt as though she was being lifted up in the air, and her companion verified that she was walking nearly a foot and a half off the ground. The next day the Elder confirmed that it was God's answer to his prayers for her safety. The Elder's concern for people was profound and, because of his suffering heart, God answered his prayers.

On Pascha,[16] 1968, Elder Amphilochios received the divine forewarning of his coming repose. He was thus given nearly two years to prepare himself and his spiritual children for his departure. He was, nevertheless, in great agony at the thought of leaving them. In tears he asked God that He allow him more time so as to encourage and develop his spiritual children. Shortly before he reposed he told one of them that the Theotokos,[17] along with St. John the Theologian, had visited him and informed him that the Lord had denied his request to remain on earth through Pascha, 1970. Soon, a bout of the flu left him very weak and his condition did not improve much. Having said his good-byes and having made final preparations for his spiritual children, he gave up his soul to his Savior on April 16, 1970.

In his essay, "The Spiritual Guide in Orthodox Christianity," Bishop Kallistos (Ware) refers to Elder Amphilochios as a contemporary example of the traditional Orthodox elder:

> What most distinguished his character was his gentleness, his humor, the warmth of his affection, and his sense of tranquil yet triumphant joy. His smile was full of love, but devoid of all sentimentality. Life in Christ, as he understood it, is not a heavy yoke, a burden to be carried with sullen resignation, but a personal relationship to be pursued with eagerness of heart. He was firmly opposed to all spiritual violence and cruelty. It was typical that, as he lay dying and took leave of the nuns under his care, he should urge the abbess not to be too severe on them: "They have left everything to come here, they must not be unhappy."
>
> Two things in particular I recall about him. The first was his love of nature and, more especially, of trees....A second thing

[16] Pascha: Orthodox Easter.

[17] Theotokos: Greek word for the Virgin Mary meaning, literally, "Mother

that stands out in my memory is the counsel which he gave me when, as a newly-ordained priest, the time had come for me to return from Patmos to Oxford, where I was to begin teaching in the university. He himself had never visited the West, but he had a shrewd perception of the situation of Orthodoxy in the Diaspora. "Do not be afraid," he insisted. Do not be afraid because of your Orthodoxy, he told me; do not be afraid because, as an Orthodox in the West, you will be often isolated and always in a small minority. Do not make compromises but do not attack other Christians; do not be either defensive or aggressive; simply be yourself.[18]

of God."

[18] Bishop Kallistos (Ware), "The Spiritual Guide in Orthodox Christianity," published in *The Inner Kingdom: Volume One of the Collected Works.* Crestwood, NY: St. Vladimir's Press, 2000, 149-50.

Elder Amphilochios of Patmos

COUNSELS

My children, I don't want Paradise without you.

Whoever plants a tree, plants hope, peace, and love and has the blessings of God.

Consider all people to be greater than yourself, though they may have many weaknesses. Don't act with hardness, but always think that each person has the same destination as we do. Through the grace of God I consider all people to be saintly and greater than myself.

The spiritual life has great joys. You fly away and leave this world and don't take anything else into consideration. You become a child and God lives in your heart.

Our country is covered with the ice of materialism and of atheism, and we are all called to take part in their defeat. Only when this ice dissipates will we be able to find and to enjoy once again that true earth which the apostolic ploughs cultivated, and which the blood of martyrs and the sweat of monastic Saints watered. Only then will the *noetic*[19] sun warm the Greek soil, which will

---

[19] *Noetic*: A Greek word referring to man's intellect. Not to be confused with man's rational faculty, the intellect is the means by which man, in a

immediately sprout forth flowers in bloom and will bear fruit, as before, to the glory of God.

With the grace of God man accomplishes his spiritual ascent, is transformed, becomes a different person, and fear leaves him. He doesn't fear death and regards this life, good though it may seem, as slavery.

Wherever Orthodox monasticism is absent, the Church does not exist, just as there cannot be a government without an army and a well-governed state without a national guard. The monastics guard the boundaries of our Church and protect Her from her enemies, who, in our contemporary materialistic age, rush to mangle Her like wolves.

God sends some people to the monastery, while others are sent by the devil. Those sent by God are sent to strengthen the monastery, while those sent by the devil are sent to dissolve it.

In order to take pleasure in the joys of monasticism and of the spiritual life, with all the powers of your soul you must cultivate prayer, patience and silence. Without prayer it is not easy to be patient, nor to be silent. With the grace of God I applied these things in my life. In this way Christ inhabits our heart.

I do nothing but sow the seeds of monasticism and of mission, though without a strategy. I pray that God will reveal the appropriate farmer to scientifically cultivate whatever I have sown, as I don't have knowledge of the art of spiritual cultivation. I see that God has now chosen Patmos as an appropriate place for a

direct manner, is able to perceive spiritual realities. It may be that Elder Amphilochios is suggesting that when man's intellect is purified of sin, it then shines like a *noetic* sun, a reflection of God, and then spiritual rebirth is possible for society, through the positive influence of man's return to God.

With Orthodox students from Uganda

spiritual airport....Distressed voices are heard from the depths of Africa that ask us for the light of Christ and for guides, so that they might also walk the holy road of Golgotha. We don't have the right to turn a deaf ear. We are obliged to open our hand to those exhausted brethren as well, as they are so far from the Orthodox Church. So, forward: fire up the spiritual factory of atomic energy!

Throughout Greece there must be hospitals for sinners, where they can stay for two or three months, according to their psychological ailments. Once they have acquired Christian experiences they would return to their work with the good habits of those spiritual establishments.

I am like the old tree in whose shade the meek sheep of Christ gather during the hot days of summer, and in whose branches the small birds gather. All ask that the old pine tree might live so that they have their joy. However, slowly, slowly its roots rot and the heavy winter will come, when a strong wind will knock him down and he will become wood for the fire. Now, however, the pine tree makes glad the sheep and birds that gather in the desert.

[The priest's cassock] is the flag of the Church of our Christ: for this reason we must try hard to honor it, we who wear it, with a holy life, so that those who don't wear it will honor and respect it.

Worldly people tire me, for whatever they have stored within them comes upon me like electric currents.

The words of preachers today have the effect of throwing turpentine on a fire.[20] The poor and unlettered laity have been abandoned and now don't listen. They need to see good works and lives of Christian love...they need to feel that their brother is co-suffering in their pain. Only through love for them and through philanthropic works will we manage to bring our brethren back close to Christ.

The egotistic person doesn't attract anyone. And if someone is attracted, that person will soon distance himself. The spiritual bond becomes indissoluble only when it meets a child-like spirit of innocence and holiness.

When man partakes of Holy Communion he receives power and is enlightened, his horizons widen, and he feels joy. Each person experiences something different, analogous to his disposition and the flame of his soul. One person feels joy and rest, another peace, another a spirit of devotion and another an inexpressible sympathy towards all things. Personally I have often

[20] The Church in Greece has specially appointed preachers who have the blessing and responsibility to deliver sermons to the faithful (thus the term "preacher" in this case has quite a different connotation than the English word does).

With Hieromonk Athanasios (Yievtich), now retired Bishop of Bosnia and Herzegovina (Serbia), a spiritual son of the great confessor of Orthodoxy, Fr. Justin Popovich. Fr. Justin corresponded with Elder Amphilochios and honored him by naming another prominent spiritual son, the present Metropolitan of Montenegro, Amphilochios, after him. On Hieromonk Athanasios's first visit to the Elder he received a sign of his holiness when he called out to him and welcomed him by name, even though they had never met, thus revealing to him the Elder's spiritual gift of clairvoyance.

felt tired, but after Holy Communion I felt myself completely renewed.

Brother, forget your sins: our Christ has blotted them out from the Book of Life.

In the hour in which we are tempted we must be patient and pray. Temptation is a clever craftsman. He is able to make small things loom large. Temptation disquiets, saddens, and creates external battles. He knows many arts. He brings man to doubt. For this reason we have many shipwrecks. When we are beset by temptations, that's when the grace of God comes. When one undergoes temptation, he recognizes his weakness, is humbled and attracts the grace of God. Don't let the winds of temptation affect you. They can't do you any harm.

Allow your soul to accept with simplicity the treasure offered in the holy texts of the Neptic[21] Fathers of our Church and try to guard it with the virtue of humility. When your study is accompanied by holy fear, you will sense divine grace.

Spiritual battles must bear the stamp of honest love and humility. Only he who bears this stamp doesn't notice the difficulties of this life, nor the villainy of satan, nor the animosity that his minions show.

Spiritual cultivation can take place only in the soil of the heart, for within it one can plant and sow spiritual seed. Then the rain

[21] *Neptic*: The adjective form of the Greek word *nepsis*, which is translated variously as "watchfulness" or "sobriety" in the spiritual life, and which expresses both of these words. The ascetic practice of nepsis involves the training of one's mind to be continuously attentive to the movement of thoughts that attempt to enter it, and thereby to distract it from prayer. For more discussion see glossary heading, *Neptic*.

of the energy of the Holy Spirit comes and brings forth fruit, which will be kept in two accounts: firstly in Heaven, and then in the earthly account for the poor and for those who hunger spiritually.

When our heart has no love for Christ, we are like ships that have no fuel, no gas in their engines. We must always remember Christ with love. Then our soul will leap for joy.

Love Christ, have humility, prayer, and patience. These are the four points of your spiritual compass. May the magnetic needle be your youthful Christian heart.

When someone opens your heart, I'd like him to find nothing there but Christ.

I ask you to put this order into practice: as much as you can, try to cultivate your love toward Christ's own person. You must reach the point that whenever you mention His name, tears run from your eyes. Your hearts must be truly ablaze. Then He will be your Teacher, your Guide, your Brother, your Father, your Elder....

Pay no attention to things earthly and passing. Be concerned about the union of your soul with God.

My child, the father confessor must cry, he must grieve, even more than the person who comes for confession, in order to relieve him. Your grief must be sincere, because the soul understands.

You should be joyful! Jesus holds a sculptor's chisel in his hands. He wants to make you into a statue for the heavenly palace.

The Jesus Prayer[22] is the foundation of perfection. There is no other way to purification and sanctification except through the Jesus Prayer. This prayer has filled Paradise with holy men and women.

Once you have cultivated the Jesus Prayer, you will become children of the palace. You will know the King's language and the ways of true royalty.

I point out the things I must, but you will profit more when, rather than my saying many words, you yourself shed two or three tears before Christ.

Man is not guilty, my child. Unfortunately, hiding underneath man's weaknesses is that hater of the good, the archenemy of God's will, the devil.

The person who doesn't have Christ sees all things as difficult and dark.

Love the One so that all will love you. Not only humans will love you, but also the mindless animals, because when divine grace appears it electrifies and magnetizes whatever it finds in front of it. However, not only will they love you, they will also honor you, for in your person will be fashioned the pure virginal face of Him Whom you love and worship.

My child, may heavenly love always fill your heart and flood it with only lofty and divine desires. Then you will relish the divine whispers of your adored Bridegroom, Who delights in conversation with you, when your heart is His throne. You must keep

[22] The Jesus Prayer: "Lord Jesus Christ, Son of God, have mercy upon me, a sinner," is the most basic and common prayer used by monks and laymen alike in the Orthodox Church.

your heart as a constant white and holy tabernacle.

I was born to love people. It doesn't concern me if he is a Turk, black, or white. I see in the face of each person the image of God. And for this image of God I am willing to sacrifice everything.

Prayer offered with diligence, vigilance, piety, faith, compunction, and care is good and beneficial. The devil, in a variety of ways, fights those who pray, while those who don't pray he loves. Man speaks to God through prayer and seeks those things that are good and salvific. The one who prays needs to be humble.

Prayer has filled Heaven with so many holy people. There is no other way of purification and sanctification apart from *noetic* prayer.[23] The psalms are good and generally all ecclesiastical hymnography. We use them, though, to attract and touch the world. We monastics, however, must speak to the King mystically. Those who chant are like those people who are outside the palace of the King and sing various songs so as to show their enthusiasm. The King is certainly pleased with these songs, as they are sung in His Honor. However, He is more attentive to the mystics of His court, those who speak into His ear.

Prayer without love is like a bird that seems good and beautiful, but, as it has no wings, can't fly.

I want to establish stations of prayer throughout our islands. I want to hear within you the voice of the Lord, for the Lord to speak from your hearts. Through prayer, become thrones of

[23] *Noetic* Prayer: Prayer that is characterized by the descent of the mind, saying the words of the Jesus Prayer, into the heart. It is intimately related to *nepsis* and *hesychasm*. For a proper treatment of the intricacies of this tradition of prayer, see *St. Silouan the Athonite*, particularly chapters six and seven, 131-171.

the Lord.

When I sit on a high rock of prayer, I am not affected, though many waves may come. However, when they find me on low rocks, they wash over me. *Noetic* prayer assimilates, binds together, and sanctifies. When the conflagration of prayer is lit in the soul, all dryness is burnt up and disappears. When prayer begins, you feel joy, then sweetness, and finally, as a fruit, come tears, for you feel the presence of Jesus.

With the prayer[24] man becomes like a child. It brings him back to the simplicity and innocence that Adam had in Paradise before the fall. With the prayer one acquires blessed, holy dispassion.[25] Through the prayer you sanctify the place you are sitting and the work you are doing. Prayer arranges all things. It enables you to walk on water. It eliminates distances between you and others. It changes the will of others. It gives courage, faith, and patience in life.

Sweeten your thoughts with good thoughts of comfort and hope. Enflame your words with the warmth of love for your Bridegroom and bring to remembrance His sufferings which He suffered for you, and thus you will remain stable, devoted and humble.

[24] The prayer: It is common in Greece for the Jesus Prayer to be referred to as simply "the prayer."

[25] Dispassion: The Elder is not referring to the destruction of man's senses, but on the contrary, to their purification and transfiguration. Dispassion "is the transfiguration of the passionate aspect of the soul...rather than its mortification. Thus dispassion in this context does not signify a stoic indifference, but rather, a transfiguration and sanctification of the powers of the soul and eventually of the body also" St. Anthony's Monastery, *Counsels from the Holy Mountain*. Florence, AZ, 1999, 423.

Precious Vessels

We must love Christ: this is necessary for the life of our soul. We also need to love God's creation: animals, trees, flowers, birds, and, above all, the most perfect of God's creation, man.

Loneliness is a conversation with God and with those spirits that approach us with love and tenderness. I will never exchange the dry and dark rocks of Patmos for the flower-lined gardens of Athens. People in the city are without a holy covering. They look at the pretty flowers and beautiful country houses, without their hearts giving thanks to God who has filled us with so many beautiful things. On the other hand, in a deserted place, even the ugliest spot and worst-sounding bird makes you sense God's nearness to you. He who is near God is most fortunate, though he might live on a rock.

Often when someone throws a rock at a dog, rather than rushing at the person who threw the stone, the dog will run and bite the stone. We do the same thing. The tempter uses someone else to tempt us, either in word or deed, and rather than deal with the tempter, who threw the stone, we bite the rock, our fellow man that the hater of the good used against us.

He who is without love cannot be called a Christian, lest we mock Christianity.

Always be attentive, pray, and study so as to cultivate your souls and scale the heights! The Church and our society are waiting for you.

Elder Epiphanios of Athens, founder of the
Monastery of the Keharitomeni (Most Graceful)
Mother of God in Trizina, in the Peloponnese

2

ELDER EPIPHANIOS

On December 27, 1930, in the small town of Vornazion in the southwestern Peloponnese, the blessed Elder Epiphanios (Theodoropoulos) was born into the world. His pious parents John and Georgia gave the name Etioklis to this their first of six children. Despite all the attention he received as the first-born child, Etioklis spurned worldly attention from an early age. He focused his attention on Christ, following the pious example of his mother and particularly of his aunt. His aunt, Alexandra, had an especially important influence on his life, a fact that Fr. Epiphanios referred to many times. In addition to playing an important role in his early education and upbringing, she also helped him during his years as an archimandrite[1] in Athens.

As a child of two he would tell people of his desire to become a priest, and donning a sheet, would play priest. From the tender age of five he attended all the services of the local church, fasting and preparing for Holy Communion in the same way as the Church prescribes for adults. One Sunday, in fact, concerned for the boy's health (he was particularly thin at the time), his aunt tried to get him to drink a glass of milk before leaving for the liturgy. The boy was visibly upset and responded, "Shall we

---

[1] Archimandrite: A Greek word meaning literally, "the head of the fold," and which refers to the abbot of a monastery. In contemporary usage, it is also a title bestowed upon a celibate priest.

go to church with a full stomach? How will we pray? How will we take *antidoron*?[2] Are we going just to listen to the service?" Etioklis would arrive early for church, often before the priest. Early one Sunday morning, the village priest went to prepare for the liturgy. On arriving at the church, he could just make out a pair of eyes looking at him in the darkness from the doorway of the church. Afraid that the person might be dangerous, he went to Etioklis's house to see if he had left for church yet. On hearing the story his aunt Alexandra laughed, "Ah! My dear father, what are you afraid of?! It's Etioklis waiting for you with lit charcoal for the censer!"

One evening, on learning that his aunts would be going to an early morning liturgy in one of the many chapels that dot the countryside, Etioklis begged them to take him with them. Despite their assurances that they would wake him, the young Etioklis sensed that they would not follow through on their word, as they had done in the past. In his zeal for the Church's services, he decided to hide his aunts' shoes so that they would be forced to wake him, and take him with them!

When he was old enough, Etioklis was sent to the school in the nearest large town, Kalamata. He was a good student and enjoyed his studies, except for mathematics. His remark to his aunt is characteristic: "What do I need math for? Am I going to become a merchant? I'm going to become a priest!" From early on in his academic career he distinguished himself by his love for study and his fine character. Both his fellow students as well as his teachers recognized this, and he was thus sought after to serve in various positions of authority and responsibility. Etioklis did not spend his time and energies in many of the normal

[2] *Antidoron*: From a Greek word meaning literally, "in place of the gifts." In English it is also called "blessed bread," and is given out to the faithful at the end of the liturgy. Here Etioklis is referring to the practice among Orthodox Christians to refrain from taking *antidoron* if one has not abstained from food completely from the night before.

pursuits of young people, but rather in reading Holy Scripture as well as the works of the Fathers. He began his theological training on his own while he was in junior high school and thus developed his belief, oft-repeated, that it is not the university that creates the scholar, but rather one's "chair," that is to say, his personal study. In addition to his academic studies, Etioklis did not neglect his spiritual development and thus spent a great deal of time not only in the Church's services, but also visiting what he called the "aristocracy" of Orthodoxy, the monasteries. In particular he would often visit the Voulcanou Monastery, located near Kalamata.

In 1949 Etioklis moved to Athens, having successfully completed his studies in Kalamata. He enrolled at the Theological School of the University of Athens, but, having a great appetite for knowledge, he didn't limit himself to the study of theology. Following the example of the Cappadocian Fathers[3] and other great Fathers of the Church, Etioklis threw himself into the study of Greek and foreign authors, philosophers, poets, historians, scholars, and apologists from ancient times to the present. In addition to his personal study, he would also attend lectures at the Schools of Law, Philosophy and Medicine, among others, so as to broaden his knowledge. Many of his professors, recognizing his intellectual gifts, encouraged him to continue his studies abroad so as to return and follow the path of university teaching. Etioklis refused, however, unwilling to sacrifice the grandeur of the priesthood for the lower path of scholarship. Instead of going abroad for graduate studies, he preferred to specialize in the "science" of the spiritual life at the "university" of the monastery. He believed that it is necessary for candidates

[3] The Cappadocian Fathers: Sts. Basil the Great, Gregory the Theologian and Gregory of Nyssa. They are renowned for the depth and breadth of their secular and religious education. Their education, combined with the holiness of their lives, enabled them to serve the Church at a particularly crucial time

for the priesthood (and especially celibate priests) to spend time in monasteries so as to better prepare spiritually for pastoral service. During his years in Athens, Etioklis frequently visited the Monastery of Longovarda on the island of Paros. The abbot of the monastery there, the blessed Elder Philotheos (Zervakos), was his spiritual father until his repose in 1980.

In the sphere of academics Etioklis's greatest love was the study of Holy Scripture. He would study the whole of the Old and New Testament from the ancient text, three times each year. He referred to Scripture frequently, using it as his main source in speaking and writing. When asked what he would have studied had theological studies not been an option, he replied medicine or law: medicine, as it is the most philanthropic science, and law, as the lawyer has the possibility of greatly affecting society by championing the good and by protecting the innocent.

In November 1956, Etioklis's childhood dream was realized when he was ordained to the diaconate by Metropolitan Ierotheos of Aitolia and Akarnania, and was given the new name Epiphanios. That same year he also published his first book, *Holy Scripture and the Evil Spirits*. The years of his diaconate were spent mostly in Kalamata, where he had the opportunity to continue his study of the Fathers as well as to spend time with important ecclesiastical personalities of his day.

Elder Epiphanios had patiently waited until after his twenty-fifth birthday to be ordained to the diaconate, so as to remain faithful to the precision of the Church's canons[4] regarding the age at which men may be ordained as deacons. Though he

in the explication of Christian doctrine.

[4] Canons: Regulations concerning ecclesiastical life and behavior. The Church's canonical tradition is a living tradition that, while insisting on fidelity to the historical expression and implementation of the canons, continues to develop with the Church, addressing contemporary needs and serving the spiritual goal of the salvation of souls.

Elder Epiphanios as a young cleric

never disregarded the need and use of Economy[5] as regards the canons, and made use of it in his pastoral service, when it came to himself, he was very strict and insisted on keeping them precisely. He was accused at various times of having a pharisaical attachment to the holy canons. His answer was that many people in the Church today, by seeking ways to reject the canons, are in fact rejecting gifts that the Holy Spirit has given the Church.

[5] Economy: From the Greek word *oikonomia*, which in this case has a deep theological meaning. The Church's use of this term derives from the "Economy" of our Lord Jesus Christ, which was His great condescension, as God, to become man in the Incarnation. Though man deserved death, God reached out to man, out of love, to save him. Both the bishop and the spiritual father, in the bending of certain Church canons, exercise Economy in the Church. According to the Fathers, Economy is properly applied as a loosening or tightening of a rule in a certain place, at a certain time, for the

His insistence on the keeping of the canons was inspired by his reverence and obedience toward the Holy Spirit Who inspired them and the Holy Fathers who wrote them.

In 1961 Elder Epiphanios was ordained to the priesthood by Metropolitan Ambrose of Eleutheropolis. The Elder followed the example of the Apostle Paul in serving the Church without pay or benefits. In order to survive, he worked as an editor of the publications of the Astir publishing house. One of his spiritual children once suggested that he get on the Church's payroll, not to earn money, but to ensure insurance and a pension. He refused, insisting that God, as a good and faithful "Employer" does not leave His "employees" without pay.

Elder Epiphanios's desire was to serve the Church in a quiet and invisible way. He was granted his wish with a position as priest of the little chapel of the Three Great Hierarchs[6]in downtown Athens. It was here that he zealously served the suffering people of God as confessor. Despite the strictness of his approach to spiritual counsel, crowds of people from all walks of life flocked to him for guidance and spiritual comfort. Although he suffered along with those who came to him, his work, at the same time brought him the greatest peace.

In addition to his work as a priest and confessor he also served the Church through the twenty-two books and many articles he wrote. His opinion was sought after by bishops, priests, monks, and laymen, to help them answer many of the complex theological and ethical problems of the contemporary world. Because of the great respect the faithful had for him, he was asked many times to become bishop, an honor that he refused.

Although Elder Epiphanios lived most of his life in the heart

salvation of a certain person or persons.

[6] Three Great Hierarchs: Sts. Basil the Great, Gregory the Theologian, and John Chrysostom.

of Athens, he managed to keep a strict rule of prayer. First thing in the morning, having said morning prayers, he would read the service of Matins along with the canons[7] from the *Menaion*[8] and from the *Paraklitiki*.[9] When his morning rule of prayer had ended he would spend time in study or writing and then begin his pastoral work, receiving guests or visiting people, according to the needs of the day. His work would barely stop for lunch, during which he would meet with people or speak with them on the telephone. At about five o'clock in the afternoon he would begin the evening services with Vespers followed by a Supplicatory Canon.[10] He would then leave for the chapel of the Three Great Hierarchs, where he would receive people for confession, after which he would visit the sick and suffering in the hospitals. On his return home there would usually be people waiting for him or telephone calls to receive. He would have a late dinner, read Small Compline[11] and the *Akathist*[12] to the Mother of God,

[7] Canons: In this case, ecclesiastical hymns based on the so-called "Old Testament Canticles," of Moses, of Miriam, and so on.

[8] *Menaion*: From the Greek word meaning "month," it refers to the twelve liturgical books (one for each month) that include the Church's hymnographical texts for each day of the year, for the feasts and Saints' days throughout the year.

[9] *Paraklitiki*: Book based on the weekly cycle of liturgical prayer, containing the hymns of resurrection (for Sundays) and hymns for each day of the week. Each day is dedicated to a different theme: Monday to the angels, Tuesday to St. John the Baptist, Wednesday and Friday to Christ's Cross, Thursday to the Apostles and to St. Nicholas, and Saturday to the martyrs and the reposed.

[10] Supplicatory Canon: A special hymn of supplication to Christ, the Theotokos, a Saint, or the angels. The Supplicatory Canon is one of the many elements of the Church's rich liturgical tradition, and are said by the faithful at any time of need or thanksgiving.

[11] Small Compline: The traditional prayers before bed said by Orthodox Christians (according to the Greek typikon). In the monasteries, the whole community usually reads it after the evening meal.

[12] *Akathist*: A service of similar use and length as the Supplicatory Canon, it

Elder Epiphanios with Archimandrite Agathangelos
(Michalidin), his spiritual father following the repose
of the blessed Elder Philotheos of Paros

and then attempt to sleep, as he suffered from insomnia.

The Elder's insomnia eventually grew so bad that he prayed for divine assistance. During one such sleepless night, he picked up the New Testament and looked for some understanding of his struggle. His eyes immediately fell upon St. Paul's Second Letter to the Corinthians, verse 12:7, "there was given to me a thorn in the flesh, the messenger of Satan to buffet me, lest I should be exalted above measure." Elder Epiphanios was grateful for God's answer to his prayer, that at least he knew his suffering was allowed by God. On two other occasions, having reached the limits of his strength, he asked God for His assistance and, opening the New Testament, immediately received the same response. Not so bold as to ask the same thing a fourth time, he simply suffered on.

In 1976, at the urging and with the help of his spiritual children, Elder Epiphanios founded the Holy *Hesychastirion*[13]of the Keharitomeni ("Most Graceful") Mother of God in Trizina, in the Peloponnese, a few hours from Athens. His hope of providing a place of monastic struggle for those of his spiritual sons who sought the monastic life was thus realized. He continued his service in the world as well, however, dividing his time between Athens and his monastery.

Not long after the foundation of the monastery, the Elder's health began to deteriorate. His demanding regime had taken its toll, and in December 1982 he was operated on in Athens. He had been suffering from stomach ailments and was diagnosed with gastrorrhagia, which in his case had the possibility of developing into cancer. The operation was very taxing on him and the surgeon ended up removing three-quarters of his stomach. The Elder's poor health continued to plague him and eventually left him in such a state that he was completely confined to his bed, unable to sit up. Having arranged for his funeral and burial he prepared himself spiritually for his repose. On November 10, 1989, at the age of 58, he gave his soul into the hands of God.

is traditionally read halfway through the service of Small Compline.

[13] *Hesychastirion:* A Greek word that denotes a place dedicated to the practice of *hesychia* which means "stillness."

"When I study the Holy Scripture and patristic books, I leave
the earth and go to Heaven....I don't manage to write my
thoughts in time, for I am flooded as with flakes
of snow. I feel as though my pen has wings."

COUNSELS

True love is like the flame of a candle. However many candles you light from the flame, the initial flame remains unaffected. It doesn't lessen at all. And every freshly lit candle has as much flame as the others do.

I want whoever is near me to feel that he has room to breathe, not that he is suffocated. I don't call anyone to me. I don't hold onto anyone. I don't chase anyone away. Whoever wants comes, whoever wants stays, whoever wants leaves. I don't consider anyone a supporter or a follower.

I am not afraid of death. Not, of course, because of my works, but because I believe in God's mercy.

Speak more to God about your children than to your children about God....The soul of the teenager is in a state of an explosion of freedom. This is why it is hard for them to accept counsel. Rather than counseling them continuously and reproaching them again and again, leave the situation to Christ, to the *Panagia*,[14] and to the Saints, asking that they to bring them to reason.

---

[14] *Panagia*: Greek word meaning "All-Holy." It is perhaps the most beloved term of endearment for the Mother of God in the Greek language.

Don't be neglectful of prayer! At table, in the morning, afternoon, and evening. In particular don't miss Small Compline for any reason, tired though you may be. It's a question of self-sacrifice and, in particular, of love. When a beloved person calls you very late at night, how are you able to speak sometimes for a few hours, despite your fatigue—without being put out, but being, rather, pleased?

Deal with your children as with colts, sometimes tightening and other times loosening the bit. When the colt kicks, without abandoning the bit, we loosen it, otherwise it will break. When, however, it is peaceful, then we tighten the bit and take the colt where we like.

Parents should love their children as their children and not as their idols. That is to say, they should love their children as they are and not how they would like them to be—to be like them.

Whoever fears God doesn't fear anything else.

I am in pain and agonize over the path of the Greek people, who are constantly being de-hellenized, de-christianized, de-colorized, cut off from their roots, and are losing their identity.

In marriage, abstention solely out of love for God is perfect, "the best."[15] When the couple comes together, not obstructing the procreation of children, it is at the level of "very good." And when they abstain solely to avoid the procreation of children, they are on the level of "good." In any case all of these categories are "above average," but are only legitimate with the presupposition that they have been agreed upon by both spouses and not just one. Otherwise it is a sin.

[15] Elder Epiphanios uses terminology from the grading system at school to make his point. "The best" is an "A," "very good," is a "B," etc.

God appointed the salvation of the world to His Son and not to us....We must first look at our soul, and, if we can, let's help five or six people around us.

When someone is free, he has rights and responsibilities. When he marries, he has few rights and very many responsibilities. However, when he has children he doesn't have any rights at all, but only responsibilities.

Why do they put rubber tires with inner tubes on cars? So that they give in, collapsing a little with every little stone or pothole in the road, and in this way they pass obstacles. If the wheels were firm and unyielding, the car wouldn't be able to move forward. It would fall apart after a short distance because of the vibration from the small inconsistencies of terrain. The same thing happens with yielding to others in the family. In this way many problems are surpassed and continuous spiritual progress is assured.

When people treat us unjustly, God justifies us.

[God allows virtuous people to suffer] so that they might be purified from even the slightest traces of their passions and so that they might receive an even greater crown in Heaven. Furthermore, as He allowed His beloved Son to suffer and to die on the Cross, what can we say for those people who, as holy as they may be, have filth and stains from sin?

Sadness purifies us. Man is truly man in sadness. In joy he is changed, he becomes someone else. In sadness he becomes that which he truly is. And this is the way, *par excellence*, that he approaches God. He senses his weakness. Many times, when he is in glory and joy, he feels that he is the "eye of the earth" or, if you prefer, the center of the universe: "I am, and nobody

Elder

75

Epiphanios

else!" In pain and sadness he feels like an insignificant ant in the universe, that he is completely dependent, and he seeks the help and companionship of God. Those of us who have passed through pains, either psychical or physical, know that we never prayed as hard and with such quality and length, as we did when we were in the bed of pain or when some heavy psychical sadness tested us. While, when we have everything, we forget prayer and fasting, and many things. It is for this reason that God allows pain.

Don't sit, glued to the television....Guard yourselves from the means of mass blinding.

We didn't come here [to the monastery] mainly for handiwork, or for the gardens or for the buildings. For even without these things we can save our soul. We came here primarily for the soul. And in order to save the soul, we must pass the day without sin, with meekness, canon,[16]and prayer.

I sacrificed everything even before I had anything. I sacrificed a place at the university as a professor. I sacrificed the position of first secretary of the Holy Synod. I sacrificed the position of director of a missionary brotherhood. I sacrificed the position of first priest of a large church. I sacrificed episcopal[17]thrones.... [A]ll I have is a little *epitrahili*[18]so as to confess ten souls. Nothing else!

There is no greater satisfaction for me than to remain for hours in the seat of the confessional and to reconcile man to God.

Married and unmarried priests, let us not forget that we are

[16] Canon: In this case, the daily rule of prayer, reading, prostrations, and so on, that a monk keeps in his room.

[17] That is, the position of bishop.

[18] *Epitrahili*: In Greek, literally, "upon the neck." It is the stole that the priest or bishop wears around his neck when hearing confession (hereafter, "stole").

representatives of the gentle and humble-hearted Jesus. We were called to progress in humility and not to quarrel in the holy altar for priority of honor.

Clerics and, in particular, celibate clerics must be chosen from those of a mature age, with excellent education, extreme piety, shining ethos, sterling character and complete spiritual formation: all those things that are acquired with labors and struggles, prayer and study, fasting and vigils, with voluntary poverty and hardships, and through various deprivations. For asceticism is not the privilege or responsibility of monastics alone, but of all the faithful and particularly of clerics, and especially of unmarried clerics. The Orthodox Church is deeply ascetic and those who don't love asceticism and who are friends of luxury and comfort don't have a place within Her.

The priest is the incarnation of the absolute, the expression of the constant, stable and unshakeable, the trumpet of Heaven, the image of incorruption, the mile-marker of eternity. May he remain forever unchanged, even in his external appearance, as a reminder and symbol of the ages and of the unchanging truths that he represents.

The priesthood is a very great gift of God toward mankind. It is the conduit of the grace of God.

It seems a blasphemy to me [an archimandrite's sadness at not having been elected bishop]. If you consider that your shell of a body can take bread and wine and, with the Holy Spirit's consecration, transform it into the Body and Blood of Christ; that you have been given the power to make the children of Adam partakers of the Cross and resurrection of Christ through baptism, and how you have been given the power to place your hands and your stole over the head of the greatest sinner and to bring him out of confession with a pure and whitened soul,

Elder Epiphanios in his study

how can you then consider yourself unsuccessful? Because you haven't put on a mitre?[19] May God have mercy on us!

I have made an agreement with God: I will empty my pockets in almsgiving and He will fill them. He has never violated our agreement. Will I violate it? May it never happen!

Ah! My fathers, know how much I have ground down my will! I have loved two things in my life: reading and writing, both of which I have been deprived of, and the deprivation of which is as great for me as for him who loses the greatest joy in this world. When I study the Holy Scripture and patristic books, I leave the earth and go to Heaven. As for my own writing, forgive me for what I'm about to say...I get drunk. I see how others desire to write some text, and they erase, write, erase again, write again.... I don't manage to write my thoughts in time, for I am flooded as

[19] Among clergy in Greece only bishops wear a mitre while serving in church.

with flakes of snow. I feel as though my pen has wings. However, in spite of my writing ability and my desire for study, I deprive myself and sit and pick up the telephone, which rings constantly, so as to find a solution to some problem or other. Or else I see people for confession for hours without end, and not only scholars, but also simple and unlettered people. In saying this I don't undervalue the Mystery of Confession as opposed to the work of writing. But the will of God was that I confess people and not that I study and write, though they much enchant me.

How crafty the devil is! To young people who managed to unite in Christian marriage he whispers, "How much better you would be if you went to the monastery and lived the heavenly spiritual pleasures, far from the cares of family life which sever you and keep you down!" While to those who went to the monastery, as they desired the life of virginity in Christ, he whispers, "How much better you would be, if you got married and made your home a temple of God, living the joys of marital life, far from ascetic mortification and the loneliness which depresses you!" And if the married one became a monk and the monk married, he would tell them the opposite. All this to throw the person into despair and to pull him from the path of salvation. For the path of salvation is both blessed marriage and virginity in Christ.

The mathematics of God is completely different from the mathematics of humans. For us two and two equal four. For God two and two can make five or fifteen or anything else.

My heart only has entrances. It doesn't have exits. Whoever enters remains there. Whatever he may do, I love him the same as I loved him when he first entered into my heart. I pray for him and seek his salvation.

My worst hell is to realize that I have saddened a beloved person.

Elder Iakovos of Evia

3

ELDER IAKOVOS

Blessed Elder Iakovos (Tsalikis) of Evia was born on November 5, 1920, in Livisi, Asia Minor (in modern-day Turkey) into a family that included seven generations of priest-monks, a bishop, and a Saint. He was baptized soon afterwards with the name of his paternal grandfather, Iakovos Tsalikis. His pious parents Stavros and Theodora suffered greatly under the Turks and in the early 1920's were forced to flee the land of their forefathers, along with the rest of the inhabitants of Livisi. At the time, Stavros Tsalikis had been taken captive by the Turks, along with many other Greeks, and forced to work on a building site in Trebizond. He did not learn until later that the Greeks of Livisi had been forced to flee. Eventually, however, by the grace of God, the family was reunited on the island of Evia, where the refugees from Livisi had been sent. The Elder recalled this traumatic time later on in life, "Despite my young age I remember, when we arrived in the port of Piraeus,[1] that we heard, for the first time, someone blaspheming divine things. My grandmother then said, 'How is it that we've come here? It would be better for us to go back and let the Turks kill us than to hear such things.' In Asia Minor we had never encountered such a sin."

The Elder looked back on his upbringing with a great sense of gratitude to his parents, and especially to his mother, who, he

---

[1] The main port of Athens.

explained, "had a monastic soul." She was very careful regarding modesty and he recalled that the family's life together was a "humble, blessed, holy, ascetic life." The children had a great love and respect for their elders and before they went to partake of Holy Communion, having prepared through strict fasting, they would kiss the hands of their parents and of the elderly of the community.

From an early age little Iakovos sensed the closeness of God and thus, even before he understood exactly what they were saying, he distanced himself from the rough children who would use foul language and act poorly. His first home in Greece was in a storehouse. Their "house" was divided from the others by blankets; there he lived with his mother and grandmother. His favorite "toy" was a little censer he fashioned out of a curved roof tile. He would go around the house censing his family and, lifting a blanket, would cense his neighbors, saying, "halujah, halujah." Every evening he would visit his favorite place, a little chapel, with his grandmother, so as to light the vigil lamps. There she would teach him the lives of the Saints and speak about the priest-monks in their family. By the age of six little Iakovos had managed to learn the Divine Liturgy by heart, including everything said or chanted by the priest and chanters on Sundays. His pious mind was like a sponge, and so he easily learnt things relating to the Church, Her faith, piety, and worship. His piety and character were such that from an early age his contemporaries gave him the nicknames, "grandpa," "monk," and "Father Iakovos."

The first schoolhouse in the town of Farakla, on Evia, was housed in the small chapel of St. Paraskevi. Iakovos loved going there; he would study there by day and go in the evening as well, so as to light the vigil lamps and to pray. One evening, when he was about eight or nine years old, St. Paraskevi appeared to him as she was depicted in her icon. Frightened, little Iakovos ran home. This happened to him again a few days later, but this time the Saint managed to calm him down. From that time on she appeared to him frequently. They would sit together in the chapel and converse.

When Iakovos learned to read, he began to spend great amounts of time studying the Church's liturgical books. By the age of nine he was already regarded by everyone in the village as one set apart for the service of God. He lived ascetically, rising in the middle of the night to pray and keep vigil. During the day he would recite Supplicatory Canons and hymns under his breath. He had a beautiful voice and chanted very well. While serving in church Iakovos was very careful and trembled at the visions he had of the angels serving at the altar. At the same time, he sensed a blessed spiritual sweetness that comforted him. From this young age he was the one entrusted with the keys of the church (as the village didn't have its own priest, but only one who came every other week from a neighboring village). The villagers sensed the closeness the boy had with Christ and His Saints, and so, when they had problems, they would come to him for help. He was called on to anoint with oil and to read prayers over the sick, women having difficulty in childbirth, the possessed, and for others in need. Iakovos was unable to continue his studies beyond elementary school, for his poor family increasingly needed his help.

One night in the early 1940's, St. Paraskevi appeared to him again, as she had been doing more frequently during that period, and warned him that the war would soon come to Greece. The plight of the impoverished refugees worsened even more with the German and Italian occupation. Starvation became a widespread phenomenon. Iakovos, now in his early twenties, always sought ways to increase his asceticism and during this period he began a fasting regime that he would undertake many times in his life. From Sunday afternoon until Saturday he would eat nothing. On Saturday he would receive Holy Communion, and later on eat a bit of bread and some olives. The only day he would

Elder Iakovos speaks with visitors after the liturgy

eat normally was Sunday. A number of times, however, due to
the difficult circumstances of the period, he would not even get
to eat over the weekend. One week, for example, a number of
starving children appeared, and another time some weakened
and disabled elderly, and he gave them whatever he had. He
suffered a great deal and often fainted from hunger. Remarkably,
however, he was able to continue working.

During this period Iakovos suffered a number of great temptations. Because of his poverty he was unable to afford shoes,

and when he went to chant in church some of the parishioners would make rude and critical comments. Upset by this, Iakovos was ready to give up chanting. One night, however, St. George, the patron of the church he was then attending, appeared to him and told him, "My child! I don't want you to leave. I want you to chant in my house just as you are!" Soon afterwards his mother, Theodora, became deathly ill. Though only forty years old, due to her many hardships, she appeared to be seventy or eighty. Four days before her death she informed her family when she would die. Her guardian angel, she explained, had prepared her beforehand. Everything took place as she foretold. Iakovos's father died a number of years later.

Before Iakovos could fulfill his childhood desire to enter a monastery, he had to fulfill his obligation to the Greek government and serve a term in the army. In 1947 he was enlisted, and served his time in Piraeus, near Athens. As in his village, the other soldiers didn't understand Iakovos and initially made fun of him. In time, however, most of them grew to respect him and would turn to him in times of need. Later on in life, some of his army companions would visit him at the monastery. Commenting on this the Elder would say, "the virtuous life always teaches and bears fruit, even if it takes years...while if I had followed them in their activities, what good could have come of it?" When the unit commander, Lieutenant-Major Polycarp Zois, heard about Iakovos, he summoned him to his office. Having tested his piety, he was impressed by his firmness of vision and faith, and took him as his personal assistant. As it turned out, Zois and his family were pious people and appreciated Iakovos very much. They eventually wanted to adopt him, as they had no children of their own, but Iakovos, holding on to the hope of eventually entering a monastery, had to refuse.

On his discharge from the army he began to work feverishly at whatever jobs he could find, so as to provide a dowry for his sister Anastasia, a responsibility that had fallen to him after his father's death. Iakovos also spent a good deal of time fixing up the chapels and shrines around his village that had fallen into disrepair since he had left for the army.

After a few years Anastasia married, and Iakovos was free to pursue his monastic vocation. The stories his grandmother had told him of his monastic ancestors who had lived in the Holy Lands had remained vivid and alive in his mind, and Iakovos planned to go there to become a monk. "However, before leaving for the Holy Lands...I considered it necessary to go to the Monastery of St. David to ask for his blessing, help, and intercessions." Later on in life the Elder recalled the significance of this visit:

> As I approached the monastery I suddenly saw the place transformed, different than I knew it when we would visit with our fellow villagers for the feast of St. David. I saw the monastery magnificent, incredibly beautiful, of a different epoch...Outside the monastery a venerable elder with a white beard was waiting for me. It was the Saint [David of Evia]. I greeted him:
>
> -Elder, what a beautiful place this is! How did this all come to be? I've never seen anything like it!
>
> -It's the republic of ascetics. Each one has his own little house.
>
> -Elder could you give me such a house as well? I'd like it very much.
>
> -My child, if you stay here, we will give you one, but you came to venerate and to leave.
>
> -Elder, I'll stay."

As soon as I gave my promise, it seemed as though the wall of the monastery opened, and the Elder went through it and then it closed again....Immediately, together with the Saint, everything was lost. There, where the republic of ascetics was, I saw the area as it was. A wild forest...I saw the monastery as it was, a ruin...Though I had gone to the monastery as a simple pilgrim, after all that, I bowed my head and gave my word to the Saint that I would serve him with all my heart.

Iakovos soon found that shepherds with their families had taken up their abode there. Three monks lived there as well, but idiorhythmically.[2] Iakovos's presence was not welcome and the monks, as well as the shepherds and their families, tried to run him off, and eventually even attempted to murder him. Iakovos was distraught, but at the same time sensed that it was God's will for him to remain there, and so he endured their persecution patiently. St. David would appear to him, giving him confidence that he was in the right place. The young abbot, Nikodemos, had initially been unable to rectify the idiorhythmic situation of the monastery as he was forced to be absent most of the time, serving as a parish priest. With the presence of Iakovos, however, he was able to force the shepherds to leave, for now the monastery had daily services. Abbot Nikodemos had Iakovos tonsured quickly, realizing his gifts and the certainty of his calling. The tonsure took place on November 30, 1952. He was then made steward of the monastery, entrusted with the keys, the monastery books, and everything, in fact, which belonged to the monastery. Soon after, as the monastery's need for a priest became increasingly evident, the unlettered but wise and good-hearted Abbot

[2] Idiorhythmic: A form of monastic organization that leaves each monk to make his own program of food, work, and services. It is generally an indication of a state of decline of the monastic life.

Nikodemos sent Iakovos to Metropolitan Gregory, the bishop of Chalkis, to be ordained. On December 18, 1952, Iakovos was ordained to the diaconate. This was followed a day later by his elevation to the priesthood.

On Fr. Iakovos's return to the monastery he began to serve the liturgy nearly every day along with all the other services. By the Metropolitan's orders, on Sundays he would serve the liturgy in various small villages. However, the persecution by the monks, and the people they gathered, did not abate. Despite Fr. Iakovos's position as steward and priest he remained in the most inhospitable of the monastery's cells.[3] It was full of such large cracks that, one winter's night, he awoke from his traditionally short sleep to find his back covered in snow. The condition of his clothing changed little after becoming a monk, and although he had finally procured a pair of boots, he had to resole them himself using the rubber from discarded car tires.

Fr. Iakovos had desired for some time to find the hermitage where St. David had lived, so as to have a refuge from the temptations of the monastery and a more peaceful place to pray. In early 1953, he went in search of the Saint's cave and was overjoyed when he found it. Although he knew he couldn't leave the monastery to live at the hermitage (for if he did it would fall apart), he decided to spend as many nights there as he could. As he explained, "I tried to struggle [in the spiritual life] secretly. I would wait for it to get dark and, when the fathers were peacefully in their cells for the night, I would open the back gate of the monastery and would start off, in the middle of the night, for the hermitage of the Saint." One moonless night he got lost and tangled up in some bushes. Bruised and scratched, he beseeched God to shown him the way to the hermitage. Out of the many stars in the heavens, "God gave me one, too," as he put it: the star lit his path and directed him to the hermitage. This happened many times, but only when it was necessary. Another

[3] Cell: The name of the room where a monastic lives.

Elder Iakovos reading prayers over the faithful

time, Fr. Iakovos asked St. David for a favor. Being timid and gentle, Fr. Iakovos was also a bit scared of the dark. He therefore asked St. David to join him in prayer in the cave, but in a form he would recognize, so that he wouldn't be frightened. The Saint answered his prayer and appeared to him in the form of Abbot Nikodemos. Together they read Supplicatory Canons, the Psalter, and prayed the Jesus Prayer.

One night, while he was praying, the cave suddenly filled with scorpions. They covered the floor, ceiling and walls. Iakovos was overcome by fear, but quickly got hold of himself and realized that this was only a temptation from the devil. Emboldened by faith in Christ, he commanded them not to move any closer. Using a small stone, he sketched a circle around him and ordered them not to pass over into the circle. He continued his prayer until dawn, no scorpion daring to disobey the words of this man of God. Another night, overcome by fatigue, Fr. Iakovos fell asleep. St. David appeared to him and, comforting him, told him to rest awhile. On awakening he was overcome with love for God and His Saints, amazed at their love and gentleness towards him. Fr. Iakovos would return to the monastery in time for the morning service. He would wash his face a bit and then ring the bell for church.

Throughout his life, Fr. Iakovos remained dedicated to his strict ascetic typikon, increasing his asceticism in times of greater temptations. In addition to his frugality in sleep and food, he would also do thousands of prostrations every night.

The devil, realizing his inability to hinder Fr. Iakovos's progress, decided to take more direct measures. In October 1954, while he was cleaning the *despotikon*,[4] a horde of monstrous demons attacked him physically. He tried to make the sign of the Cross and to cry out to the Mother of God, but each time a demon would stop him. He was beaten mercilessly. Finally he managed to free one of his hands so as to make the sign of the Cross. The demons immediately jumped out the window. It took sometime before Fr. Iakovos was able to stand up and stumble to his room. This happened a number of other times, leaving Fr. Iakovos increasingly frail.

Fr. Iakovos suffered much physically. From an early age he had serious back problems, and problems with his tonsils, kidneys, and prostate, along with other illnesses. These were exacerbated

[4] *Despotikon*: The room where bishops and other dignitaries stay while visiting a monastery.

by his strict asceticism and the physical attacks of the demons. For many years he refused to accept any medical attention. Finally in 1967, at the age of 47, he suffered so intensely that he fell unconscious from his pain. He was taken to the hospital and eventually the doctors and priests managed to convince him to have an operation to fix what they thought was simply appendicitis, but which turned out to be much more dangerous and complex. After prayer to Sts. David and John the Russian,[5] Fr. Iakovos was taken into the operating room. Before falling unconscious from the anesthetic he saw the two Saints entering. This was just the first of many visits he would have to make to the hospital for various operations. His most serious ailment was his heart condition, which caused him excruciating pain in the chest, and often resulted in seizures.

As time went on and his condition got worse, the doctors, as well as the younger monks who had come to join him in the monastery, tried to convince him to lessen his asceticism for the sake of his bodily health. Although he appreciated their love and concern, he refused.[6] Elder Iakovos continued to grow in virtue and people were increasingly drawn to him as to a source of water in the desert. Soon after his elevation to the priesthood he had received the blessing to be a spiritual father, and thus to

[5] St. John the Russian: One of the most beloved Saints of Greece, whose relics are preserved on the island of Evia, within an hour's drive of the Monastery of St. David. Throughout his life Elder Iakovos had an especial love for St. John and made a point of venerating his relics whenever the opportunity arose.

[6] This insistence on remaining faithful to one's ascetic struggle in the face of bodily pain is a common theme throughout the lives of the Saints as well as in the lives of contemporary elders. Many people, living completely according to the logic of this world, refuse to accept this voluntary struggle as beneficial and glorifying to God. Nevertheless, there are countless references to extreme asceticism throughout Holy Scripture, in the lives of the Prophets, the Apostles, St. John the Baptist, and even Christ Himself. (cont.d) >>>

hear confessions. He would serve the people tirelessly, to the point of his own near collapse.

He was increasingly sought after for confession, counsel, healing, and exorcisms. He would pray over an afflicted person and make the sign of the Cross over the person with the skull of St. David, and the person would leave, his ailment healed. The Elder protected himself from the temptation of pride by attributing any miraculous healings to the grace of the Saint in his relic.[7] Elder Iakovos's relationship with St. David was particularly close. He spoke with him as with an older brother, at times demanding his intercession for those in sickness and distress.

Having rebuilt the Monastery of St. David, chosen his successor, and brought healing and comfort to thousands of suffering souls, Elder Iakovos was prepared for his departure from this world. He prayed to St. David that he accompany his soul on its way and told one of his spiritual children that he would

The asceticism found in these lives is unique, just as the elders whose lives are presented are unique. The question of asceticism is a completely personal one based on the completely free relationship between man and God. There are no formulas for ascetic endeavor (although there is a generally accepted framework, as regards fasting in particular), and in the Orthodox Church each of the faithful takes counsel of his or her spiritual father as to how to approach the matter of asceticism. For more discussion of the question of asceticism, please see the glossary heading, *Asceticism*.

[7] The Church teaches that the uncreated grace of God permeates both a Saint's soul and his body, during the Saint's deification, remaining with the Saint's relics even after death. The Church's experience of God's grace through the relics of His Saints, has remained unchanging throughout the two thousand years since Christ's coming. There are numerous passages in Holy Scripture that attest to this as well (2 Kings 13:21, Acts 19:11-12, to name just a few). For more on this topic, see Elder Cleopa Ilie's book, *The Truth of Our Faith: Discourses from Holy Scripture on the Tenets of Christian Orthodoxy*. Thessalonica, Greece & London, Ontario: Uncut Mountain Press, 2000, 95-105.

"depart like a bird." On November 21, 1991, having celebrated the feast of the Entrance of the Theotokos into the Temple, and having received a number of his spiritual children for confession, he gave up his soul peacefully. Although only a few calls were made to the outside world, the news of his repose spread like wildfire and faithful around Greece wept over the loss of their spiritual father in Christ. Thousands of the faithful left their jobs and families to be at Elder Iakovos's funeral. The roads to the monastery were blocked by traffic. The police arrived so as to try to keep some semblance of order. Near the end of the burial service, the huge crowd of faithful made bold to cry out, "A Saint! You are a Saint!" Since the time of his repose, blessed Elder Iakovos has continued to intercede on behalf of the faithful, and to manifest by divine signs the boldness he has attained before the face of God.

Elder Iakovos in his customary place
of prayer during the daily Divine Liturgy

COUNSELS

When I first went to the monastery, because of a fire, the mountains surrounding the monastery were mostly bare except for a few pine and fir trees. As I went to do various chores for the monastery I had in my pocket seeds from pinecones and would plant them in the whole area. At the same time I prayed for the protection of the forest, particularly from fires, which are caused by the hatred of the devil, who inspires his people to destroy the forests.

We are not sanctified by the place in which we live, but by the way we live. We may be on the Holy Mountain but, in our thoughts, be in the world. Or we may be here [in the world] in body, but *noetically* on the Holy Mountain. If someone is a proper monk, wherever he goes is the Holy Mountain.

[Keep the monastery open continuously,] for it isn't right that pilgrims wait out in the cold, in the rain, or in the sweltering heat. This is love. The monk must make a sacrifice. The monastery is not our own. We are guests here in the Monastery of St. David. We are tenants and administrators. Everything belongs to the Saint. Even the clothes we wear and the food we eat are his. The only things we brought with us to the monastery are our sins; it is for these that we have wept until now.

When we put on the cassock, we begin with the goal of sanctifying our soul. Care is necessary, however. For love of the world's honor and glory, our egotism can make us lose our soul, rather than sanctify it.

Don't be proud, my child, that when you received Holy Communion today your face shone like the sun. Even in good changes one must guard himself from pride.

Priests' wives must live a holy, nearly monastic life, with great reverence toward the priest, and must dress very modestly.

A person with an obstacle[8] to the priesthood should under no circumstances be ordained. I saw a priest who had received the permission of a spiritual father [to be ordained] without having honestly confessed, and after four years he confessed his sin to me, which was an obstacle to the priesthood. His face, black and saddened, had no joy in it. His situation saddened me greatly.

Television—the devil's box—does great harm, especially to children. For this reason it must be taken out of the house.

People are blind and don't see what takes place in church during the Divine Liturgy. Once I was serving and I couldn't make the Great Entrance[9] because of what I saw. I suddenly felt someone

[8] The word Elder Iakovos uses for "obstacle" is *kolima*, which is a special term used for something which, according to the Church's canons, makes ordination impossible (particularly serious sins such as fornication or murder). Because of these prohibitions, the blessing of one's spiritual father is necessary before one may be considered for ordination.

[9] Great Entrance: The beginning of the second part of the liturgy, during which time the unconsecrated gifts are processed around the church from the holy *prothesi* (see below) to the holy altar in anticipation of their consecration.

pushing me by my shoulder and guiding me toward the holy *prothesi*.[10] I thought it was the chanter. I turned around and saw a huge wing that the archangel had laid on my shoulder, and that he was guiding me to make the Great Entrance. What amazing things take place in the altar during the Divine Liturgy!...Sometimes I can't handle it, and so I pass out in a chair, and so some concelebrators[11] conclude that I've got something wrong with my health, but they don't realize what I see and hear.

The merciful heart [of my mother] was such that she would even give away the clothes that we needed.

When you see a shrine, make the sign of the Cross and call upon the Saint who is honored there, for the Saints are there and their grace helps us.[12]

The faithful shouldn't tell others of things they have confessed, of details of their life or their spiritual endeavor.

When the priest cuts out sections [of bread] and commemorates the names of the faithful during the *prothesi*,[13] an angel of

---

[10] Holy *Prothesi*: A small table to the left of the holy altar where the preparation of the gifts takes place before the Divine Liturgy begins.

[11] Concelebrator: One who serves (celebrates) the liturgy together with the main priest.

[12] The Elder is referring to the many small shrines set up around Greece, sometimes in memory of someone who has died, or as thanksgiving for someone who was saved from death. As a young man Elder Iakovos took it upon himself to care for the shrines by keeping them clean and in good shape, and by keeping their vigil lamps lit.

[13] *Prothesi*: Elder Iakovos is referring here to the preparation of the bread that will be used for Holy Communion. This preparation takes place before the liturgy begins. As the priest prepares the bread, he says special prayers and commemorates Orthodox Christians, living and reposed.

the Lord descends and takes this commemoration and places it before the throne of Christ as a prayer for those commemorated.

When I cut the bread in preparation for Holy Communion, I see souls passing in front of me and they ask me to commemorate them. Even if I wanted to, I wouldn't be able to forget them.

We must take care of our health, for God has given us doctors and medicine and we mustn't be indifferent.

[To parents who asked what to do when their children don't listen:] Pray with faith, counsel them as much as possible with love, in a gentle way. For, forgive me, nothing good comes of being strict. This is because they will up and leave...and today we live in Sodom and Gomorrah and worse.

We must be very careful what we ask of God in prayer, for we don't know, when we ask for a trial and He gives it, if we'll be able to bear it.

Priests shouldn't cut their hair. In Asia Minor, when priests would comb their hair, they would put a white cloth down and whatever strands of hair fell, they would gather, put them in a little bag, and when they died, they would bury it with them. This is because, when the Holy Spirit descends during ordination, the priest is sanctified; even his hair is sanctified.

An uncountable amount of money has passed through my hands, but all of it has gone to where it was meant to go, to those who suffer, to the poor, to those in need. Every month I give food, money, and whatever is necessary to families in need. I give one and God gives me ten.

Elder Iakovos in prayer

At the beginning of my priestly life in the monastery the celebration of a daily liturgy was added to the typikon of the daily
services. In the deep morning we would begin the service, and
before the sun had risen completely we would finish the liturgy.
Partaking thus daily of the Immaculate Mysteries, I felt so much
power within me that I was like a lion. My soul had such a divine
fire that all day long I didn't feel hungry, thirsty, hot, or cold.
From the morning until night I worked without rest. Even at
midday in the summer, while the other fathers were resting in
their cells looking for a bit of cool, I would carry heavy loads of
dirt and fertilize the gardens that I cultivated outside the walls
of the monastery.

I asked God in prayer to give me the gift of discerning men's
hearts by looking at their faces, so that I might be able to help
them; and God granted it.

When I give Holy Communion to people, I never look at
their faces. Occasionally, however, I have the thought to look

into the faces of those who are coming to partake. Then I see that the face of one has the form of a dog, another the form of a monkey, while others have different forms of animals, really frightening. "My God," I exclaim, "as they are humans, how do they have the faces of animals?" There are also a few who come to partake with a peaceful and bright countenance, and as soon as they partake their faces radiate as the sun.

Don't hesitate [to come to confession]. Don't be ashamed. Whatever you may have done, even the greatest of sins, the spiritual father has power from the Lord Christ Himself and from the Apostles to forgive you with his stole.

I had the habit of going to funerals and of visiting my village's cemetery. This didn't, of course, mean that I was at all melancholy or had some kind of psychological problem. I would go and philosophize on the vanity and transitory nature of this life, and the memory of death began to live in my soul.

When my elder, Nikodemos, reposed, I asked in my prayer where his soul had gone. Then I saw, not in a dream but in a spiritual way, my elder call to me to bring him the keys of the monastery, because the Great High Priest had come. So I went outside the door of his room, which is over the entrance to the monastery, and when I got close, I could hear exchanges: question, answer. An interrogation was going on inside. I knocked on the door and went into the room and what did I see!...My elder was standing, bareheaded, with his head down and his hands crossed with much fear and reverence. Opposite him was the Great High Priest sitting on a throne. The throne was hovering three feet above the ground. His face shone; golden, like pure wax—I can't describe it, my child. On His knees a book was open, and inside the life of my elder was written down. The Great High Priest asked questions and my elder responded. When I entered the interrogation stopped, and I went to my elder, bowed and gave him the keys of the monastery....I saw, my child, that our whole life: works, words, thoughts...are written down. We will have to answer for everything. As for my elder, I learned that his soul did fine.

Chase away the bad thoughts and fantasies that the devil presents. Don't even notice them.

[As a boy] I was happy to get out of the house, to walk out of the village to the nearby mountains where I would find or dig small caves for myself. There I would cut some branches off of bushes and lay them on the ground, covering them with an old blanket so as to kneel. I would pray there for hours.

My mother's soul was unique. My mother, because of my weak constitution, called me "autumn bird."

I suffer along with the person who is confessing. I feel pain along with him. I suffer and cry for him. I ask St. David that after confession I might forget whatever isn't needed and remember those things that are necessary for me to remember in prayer. I pray for the repentant; I am concerned about him and wait for him to come again.

No prayer, my children, gets lost. Prayer has sustained me for so many years.

Elder Joseph the Hesychast, cave-dweller of Mount
Athos and spiritual grandfather of countless
monks in Greece, America, and Canada

4

ELDER JOSEPH

The blessed Elder Joseph the Hesychast was born in 1898, on the island of Paros. His pious parents George and Maria gave him the name Francis in baptism. His father died young and left the family poor; but his mother, with the help of the children, who worked from a young age, managed to raise them in the fear of God. When Francis eventually left to become a monk she recounted the story of his birth, when the roof of the house disappeared and an angel descended, explaining to her that he had been given the order to take the child. From that time on, she realized that little Francis would one day serve Christ.

Francis worked in his village until he was old enough to go further afield, so as to find better work. He found a job in Piraeus, near Athens, and in addition developed his own business, becoming successful in quite a short period. A number of years later, when he was 23 years old, he began a serious study of the works of the Fathers. He was particularly impressed by the lives of the Ascetic Fathers. It was a dream he had one night, however, which gave him the decisive push towards monasticism. In the dream, two officers led him to the palace of the king. There he was clothed in a costly white robe and told that from that time on he would serve there in the palace. He was then led to reverence the king. Francis was greatly affected by this dream and decided to follow the monastic path. In search of a quiet place to pray and to live in asceticism, he fled the city, living for some time in desert places. During this period the desire to go to the Holy Mountain arose in him, and, on a trip to Athens, he met a monk from Mt. Athos who agreed to bring him back with him on his return.

On arriving at the Holy Mountain, Francis first stayed with the brotherhood of the famous Elder Daniel of Katounakia in the southern "desert" of Mt. Athos. He didn't remain there long, however, as his soul yearned for the greater silence and stricter asceticism of the deep desert. He eventually found a spot to live and pray in Vigla, a desert near the Monastery of the Great Lavra. Zealous to remain faithful to what he had read in the lives of the ancient Ascetic Fathers of the Church, Francis became disappointed by the indifference and lack of spiritual fervor he encountered in many of the monks he met. He was anxious to preserve his spiritual freedom, and not put himself under obedience to an elder immediately, until he found a monastic setting in which he would be free to pray, live ascetically and develop as much as possible.

He grew increasingly disappointed and beseeched God to help him find his way. One day he was particularly afflicted by temptations, and after much prayer and weeping collapsed from hunger and exhaustion. From where he was he looked up towards the church of the Transfiguration on the peak of Athos and sensed a gust of wind come from there, filling his heart with a divine fragrance. At the same time, he sensed the Jesus Prayer enter into his heart and pray there on its own. He was taken up into divine vision and beseeched God not to return him to earth. From that time on Francis sought solitude and silence even more diligently, cultivating the great gift God had bestowed on him. He survived by fashioning brushes out of bushes, which he brought to the Monastery of the Great Lavra, where he exchanged them for rusks of bread. He would live on them for some weeks.

That summer, for the feast of the Transfiguration, he ascended the peak of Mt. Athos, to the chapel of the Transfiguration. There, monks from all over Athos, along with pious laymen, gather for the feast. It was during this feast that Francis met Fr. Arsenios, a monk of the *Great Schema*, who would become Francis's co-struggler in asceticism. They spoke for some time and agreed upon the basic structure of the monastic regime they would follow. Afterwards, they hastened to consult Elder Daniel at Katounakia, to receive his guidance and blessing on their endeavor. When Fr. Daniel was convinced of the seriousness and surety of their intent, he encour-

Elder Arsenios

aged them and advised them to establish their life on the sure foundation of obedience to an elder. He asked them if they had an elder, explaining that without the blessing of an elder no spiritual endeavor can prosper. He suggested that they find an aging monk and put themselves under obedience to him. After the period of obedience, when the monk had passed away, they would have the blessing of God to continue to live as they hoped to. They joyfully received the Elder's words as a revelation from God to them, and zealously heeded them.

Soon after leaving Fr. Daniel the two young ascetics found their elder, Ephraim, at the nearby hermitage[1] of the Annunciation. The aging Fr. Ephraim was overjoyed with his two young disciples and did all he could not to hinder their zeal

---

[1] The Greek word *kelli* is used to refer both to the room where a monastic lives (which we rendered earlier as "cell") and to a monastic dwelling, similar to a hermitage, housing one or more monks. In this second meaning, we render the word as "hermitage."

for the monastic life. There were temptations, of course, which came mostly from the monastics living nearby, whose habits and way of life infringed on the silence and seclusion the two young ascetics desired. Elder Joseph's solution was to create a small cave for himself under an overhanging rock, with boards at the sides. After sundown he would go there for six hours, so as to dedicate himself more fully to prayer. The Elder was completely dedicated to prayer and, being completely uncompromising in his regime, would not allow anything to hinder it.

One feast day Elder Ephraim and Fr. Arsenios went to a vigil at a nearby hermitage, as they were accustomed to do. Elder Joseph however, dedicated to his regime, stayed behind in his little cave. While praying there, he was overcome once again by the grace of God. He was filled with light and beheld three beautiful young children approaching him. They walked together at the same speed, with the same rhythm, as though they were one, and yet they were distinctly three. They melodiously sang the verse, "As many as have been baptized into Christ have put on Christ, Alleluia." When they got to the word "Alleluia" they would bless him with their little hands, the way a priest does. This experience encouraged and inspired the Elder to seek even greater silence and solitude to cultivate his gift of prayer. It was decided soon afterwards, regarding the young ascetics' desire for greater silence, that rather than cause problems with the other fathers of Katounakia, it would be better if the three monks moved to a more isolated spot. Before leaving Katounakia, Elder Ephraim gave Fr. Joseph the Great Schema during the service of monastic tonsure in the cave of St. Athanasios.

The brotherhood moved to St. Basil's, higher up the mountain from Katounakia. While this provided them with greater silence, life became, practically speaking, more difficult. They built small huts for themselves, but after the blessed repose

The interior of the hermitage of St. Basil

of their elder they decided to leave them during the summer months, when they would travel from place to place, seeking silence, anonymity and spiritual guidance from spiritually mature elders. They spent most of their time around the peak of Athos and in the land further down the mountain, though they would occasionally go further afield if spiritual benefit was to be had. On their journeys they would travel light, carrying a bag for rusks, a fur-lined cassock which could be worn as well as serve as bedding, and a cooking pot which they used to cook wild plants. They did all they could to preserve silence, avoiding unnecessary encounters and walking and sitting apart from one another as much as possible. They would return to St. Basil's for the winter and remain there until Pascha. They were completely dependent on God for their food and other material needs, not doing handiwork (though Elder Joseph was gifted at woodcarving). They continued this regime for about eight years, after which they stayed in their huts continuously.

Soon after settling at St. Basil's, Elder Joseph was blessed with another divine visitation, one which would greatly affect his spiritual struggle. He found himself surrounded by the Uncreated Light.[2] He saw a battlefield with an army of monks on one side and an army of grotesque black figures on the other. A tall, noble general approached him and asked if he would like to fight in the front line. Elder Joseph eagerly replied in the affirmative. The general placed him there, and inspired him with words of encouragement. When the vision was over, the Elder began to realize the import of the vision, and prepared himself for the warfare he had willingly accepted.

One of the greatest battles he was to fight was against the passion

[2] Uncreated Light: The light of Divine Being that appeared to the disciples on Mt. Tabor (Matthew 17:1-9), and that has been experienced by the Church's Saints throughout the history of Christianity. In the fourteenth century St. Gregory Palamas zealously defended the existential experience of the

of fornication. Considering his absolute chastity and virginity (he was raised in a pious and traditional Greek family, far from the immorality of our age), coupled with the austerity of his life and prayer, the violence of the battle he waged attests to its supernatural character. After eight years of battling with this passion, Elder Joseph saw that his endurance and strength were waning. One day the Elder was sitting in his cell praying, "wounded, despairing, and virtually dead," as he recounts, when he heard the door open and someone enter. He soon became aware of someone arousing his lower members, and looking down he saw the filthy spirit of fornication that had been tormenting him for so long. Its form was as the Fathers describe: dirty, bald, with horns, wicked red eyes, and a body covered with bristles like a wild boar. He attacked the demon, just barely managing to touch its slimy, rough body, stinking of sulfur, before it escaped. From that time on the Elder sensed the burdens of that battle leave him and felt like a small child, free of the passions of the flesh.

On another occasion Elder Joseph went out one moonlit night, to confess to Elder Daniel and to receive Holy Communion. When he arrived he waited outside on a rock, so as not to disturb Elder Daniel's vigil. As he sat, saying the prayer, he began to hear the beautiful song of a bird, and his mind was enraptured by its voice. He followed the sound, searching for the bird, but in another state, which human words are unable to properly describe. He entered a meadow and continued along a pure white road, bordered by crystalline walls containing golden flowers. Overcome by the majesty of the place, he forgot about the bird, and eventually came upon a large and beautiful palace. In the door to the palace stood the Virgin Theotokos holding the Christ Child in her arms. He approached her and kissed her with great love and devotion. She embraced him and spoke to him, warming him with her motherly love. Eventually he left her, following a different road back to the meadow, where he found a beautiful mansion. He was given a gift there and was told that he was in the bosom of Abraham. He continued along and came back to himself, on the rock he had been standing on.

After his experience Elder Joseph decided to go immediately to venerate the icon of the Mother of God in the cave of St. Athanasios the Athonite. With a heart full of joy, love, and gratitude, he went to thank her for her blessing. In the cave he was once again overcome by a beautiful fragrance, as a gust of fresh air, which emanated from the mouth of the Theotokos. It enraptured him a second time, until someone came to the cave, and he fled so as to avoid questions.

The two brothers continued in their ascetic struggle at St. Basil's, leaving infrequently to visit the peak of Athos for the sake of greater silence. Fr. Joseph's reputation as a gifted elder spread, and people came to him for guidance. In addition, some came to stay, but usually proved to be more of a temptation than a blessing, as they found it difficult to adapt to the Elder's strict rule, and had difficulty surpassing their worldly habits. During this period the two elders began to work more at handicrafts. This was facilitated by their decision to stay more or less rooted at St. Basil's. Elder Joseph crafted little wooden crosses, though he was obviously capable of greater works. Even in his handiwork he was careful to keep matters simple, realizing that more intricate work would invite temptations: increased contact with the world, the need for more specialized tools, and so on. The elders thus produced just enough to buy the few supplies they required.

Despite their prudence, the elders soon felt overburdened by the cares of the world that continued to encroach. For this reason they decided to search for another more secluded spot that would give them the freedom for prayer and silence they had lost. This is how they came to hear about some empty caves that had once housed Russian monks, near Little St. Anne's Skete,[3] and, in January 1938, they took their few possessions and set up a humble hermitage there. The beginning was very

The hermitage at Little St. Anne's Skete

difficult, and Elder Arsenios bore the brunt of the work, as Elder Joseph was increasingly frail. Once they had fashioned their dwelling, they returned to their rule of life. In the mornings they would work and receive guests, after which they would shut the gate and keep silence for the rest of the day. Despite his increasingly poor health the Elder refused to yield to the weakness of his body, faithfully keeping to his rule of prayer, fasting and vigil. Eventually, a small brotherhood of young men who were able to truly benefit from the Elder, rather than hinder him, developed around him. Despite the influx of new brothers, the

Uncreated Light, understood to be an Uncreated Energy of God.

[3] Skete: A type of monastic organization somewhere between a coenobitic monastery and a hermitage. In a skete a group of small monastic dwellings are located around a central church. Generally speaking, each dwelling houses one to three monks and operates as an independent unit, except for a certain amount of common life of prayer in the central church, at least on Sundays,

Elder remained zealous in his ascetic struggle and in his general principle of keeping things simple, so as not to develop cares which would detract from the spiritual life.[4]

The Elder's concern for the younger brothers, whose health suffered from the severity of their environment, convinced him to search for a spot better suited to their regime. Their first move was to a building in New Skete, which was soon followed by a second move to some huts just outside the skete, as life in the skete proper proved to be too disruptive. These new surroundings turned out to be conducive to their regime, and the brothers did all they could to preserve silence and stillness, realizing that the Elder had sacrificed his hesychastic life near Little St. Anne's Skete for them. The move had a beneficial effect on the younger brethren, though the Elder's health continued to deteriorate. He was soon on the verge of death, suffering from benign anthrax that attacked his neck. He was initially insistent

but at some sketes more often.

[4] The great zeal of the Elder for precision and spiritual purity was not limited to the ascetic struggle, but extended to ecclesiastical matters of the day. Early on, in the years following the New Calendar innovation of Patriarch Meletios Metaxakis in 1923, Elder Joseph, along with many other ascetics in the deserts of Mount Athos, including his spiritual son Elder Ephraim of Katounakia, not only remained with the traditional ecclesiastical calendar (as did all of Mount Athos), but also joined those who separated themselves from communion with those who accepted the change. The matter was often a point of contention and disturbance among the ascetics. The Elder, however, was not one to find answers to such questions in books, but rather in prayer. Once, being troubled in spirit about his allegiance to the more extreme of the Old Calendarist groups of the time, the Matthewites, he prayed and received a vision that eventually led to his and his brotherhood's (including Elder Ephraim of Katounakia's) return to communion with the monasteries and the Orthodox who had not separated from the Patriarchate of Constantinople and from the official Church of Greece. See *Elder Ephraim of Katounakia*. Mount Athos, Greece: Holy *Hesychastirion* of Saint Ephraim, 2004.

that no medical treatment be sought, ready and willing to end his earthly sojourn. He did, however, finally yield his will to the will of his disciples. They brought in doctors who managed to lengthen his life by a year. A heart condition, however, developed unnoticed, and eventually, on the feast of the Dormition of the Theotokos, August 15, 1959, the blessed Elder reposed in the Lord, having partaken of the Holy Mysteries that morning. In this way the Theotokos proved faithful to the promise she had once made to him in a vision, when she said, "Let him place his hope in me."

Elder Joseph's life and legacy are a testament to the effect the life of one man, completely dedicated to God, may have on the whole world. Though the Elder was cut off from the world and consciously shunned the vanity of worldly glory, people were attracted to the sweetness of his life like bees to a flower. Although few were able to heed his words in their fullness, his dedicated and faithful brotherhood managed to learn from him and to disseminate his word throughout the world. When the brotherhood dispersed after the Elder's repose, his disciples shared their spiritual nectar with many others, initiating a rebirth of the spiritual life on Mt. Athos which in turn has, nearly fifty years later, spread outside the monastic republic into Greece and beyond.[5]

---

[5] Numbered among Elder Joseph's disciples are Elder Charalambos of blessed memory, abbot of Dionysiou, Elder Ephraim of Philotheou and St. Anthony's Monastery in Arizona, and Elder Joseph of Vatopaidi.

Elder Joseph with other ascetics and his brotherhood in New Skete,
including: (standing) Fr. Charalambos (former
abbot of Dionysiou), far left; Fr. Joseph (elder of Vatopaidi),
fourth from left; Fr. Ephraim the elder (of Philotheou and St.
Anthony's Monastery, Arizona), far right; (sitting) Elder Arsenios,
Elder Joseph, Fr. Theophylaktos.

(Photograph from *Athos: Heaven and Earth*,
The Holy Monastery of Philotheou).

COUNSELS

How souls might be saved...is my yearning, the fire of my heart, the divine love within, which continually burns me up inside.

Don't fear sicknesses, even when you suffer up to the edge of death. As God is constantly present, why do you worry? "In Him we live and move." Our struggle is in His embrace. We breathe God, we are surrounded by God, we touch God, we mystically eat God. Wherever we turn, wherever we look, God is everywhere: in Heaven, on earth, in the abyss, in wood, in rocks, in your mind, in your heart. So doesn't He see what you bear? That you suffer? Tell Him your complaints and you will see...healing both in your soul and in your body.

For the time being I live in a cave. I have wonderful stillness. I am the luckiest of men, for I live without cares and enjoy the honey of stillness unceasingly. And when grace departs for just a little, stillness comes as another grace and it shelters me in its harbor. And thus, the pains and sadness of this evil and tiring life seem less significant. In the present life, until one's final breath, sadness always comes mixed with joy.

If the grace of God doesn't enlighten man, though you say many words, they won't be beneficial. The person listens to you for a moment, but soon after returns to that which holds him captive.

If, however, grace works immediately, together with your words, then a change is effected at that moment, corresponding to the person's predisposition. And from that moment on, his life is changed. This happens with those who haven't hardened their hearing and conscience. On the contrary, if you speak day and night to those who hear about the good, but who disobey and remain in their evil desires, even if you give them all the wisdom of the Fathers, do miracles before their eyes, turn the flow of the Nile upon them, there's no way they will benefit in the slightest. They want, however, to come here to my hut to speak, so as to pass their time because of their listlessness. For this reason I close my door and I, at least, am able to benefit from silence and from prayer.

Question yourself as to whether this faith is within you, or perhaps you are led by worldly wisdom. And if you leave all things in the hands of God, behold! You have acquired faith and undoubtedly, without any question, you will find God to be your helper. And so, even should you be tried a myriad of times and should satan tempt you to abandon faith, prefer death a thousand times more and don't obey worldly wisdom. In this way the door of the mysteries will be opened to you and you will be amazed how the chains of worldly wisdom previously bound you. Now you will fly with divine wings above the earth and breathe the new air of freedom, which, of course, others are deprived of. If, however, you see that within you, you are governed by worldly wisdom, and in the smallest danger you lose hope and despair, know that you have not yet acquired faith, and consequently also hope, in God.

No sacrifice is more fragrant in the sight of God than purity of body, which is realized through blood and great struggles.

The farmer plows the earth, cleans, sows seed, and awaits the mercy of God. If God doesn't send rains and helpful winds when they are necessary, the farmer's toils are in vain. It's the same with us. If God doesn't send the purifying waters of His grace, we remain devoid of fruit and our works become the fodder of demons. For our passions drown them and we don't harvest anything. We mustn't forget that virtuous deeds that are not done for the right reason become evil deeds.

[The powers of darkness] are not fought with sweets and Turkish Delight, but with conduits of tears, with pain of the soul until death, with extreme humility and great patience, with unceasing painful prayer.

The enemy is found entrenched and fully armed at all three points which constitute man: soul, body, and environment. He doesn't miss any opportunity to pressure man and to test his faith. The devil, according to each circumstance, attacks and opposes our decisions. His main goal, however, is to hurt our faith and to humiliate man as a traitor and denier. If he manages to do this, he dampens man's desire and zeal. Everything takes place for the sake of faith, but, at the same time, faith upholds all things. If faith is shaken, then all things quiver and the front line bends.

The helping of others, the giving of alms, and all external goods don't calm the arrogance of the heart. Humility of the mind, the pain of repentance, and the breaking of the will, however, humble the proud spirit.

There are those who have soft souls and are easily convinced. There are also those who have hard souls and don't yield easily. The difference is as great as that between cotton and iron. The cotton requires only an anointing with words. The iron requires fire and a furnace of temptation to be worked. The man who has a hard character needs to be patient in enduring temptations for there to be a cleansing. When he isn't patient he is like a lamp without oil, which quickly goes out, and is lost.

When the mind takes possession of the prayer and man senses the joy therein, then the prayer will begin to pray continuously, on its own, without the person's struggle. Whether the person is eating, walking, sleeping or waking, he shouts the prayer within and has peace and joy. When the energy of the prayer continues for a long period, it becomes Paradise within man. He is freed from the passions and becomes a different person. If he happens to be in the desert...my! my! Then the joys of the prayer are beyond words.

Prayer offered without attention and nepsis is a waste of time, it is struggle without reward. We must set up circumspection as an unsleeping guard of all our senses, internal and external. For without attention, the mind and the powers of the soul are dispersed in vain and common things, just as useless water runs out into the road. No one can ascend to the heights unless he disdains the things below. Often when we pray our mind goes from one thing to the next, wherever it likes and to whatever it has grown accustomed to be drawn to. For this reason violence is needed for us to gather our mind and to speak the words of prayer with care.

The mind feeds the soul, and whatever good or bad thing it sees or hears it passes on to the heart, which is the center of the spiritual and physical powers of man.

Before temptation has the opportunity to draw the tempting thought into your mind, destroy it with the prayer. Don't let it be!

The Brotherhood at New Skete shortly before the Elder's repose

Flee from bad thoughts as from a fire. Don't take notice of them at all, so they can't take root in you; and don't despair, for God is great and forgives sinners. When you err, repent and force yourself not to repeat the offence.

[From a letter to a spiritual son:] Come now my beloved son, if only for a day. We will speak with God and about God. Come and enjoy Him Whom you miss. Listen to the wild boulders, those secret and silent theologians, while they develop deep thoughts for you and guide you, mind and heart, to the Creator. After Spring it is beautiful here, from holy Pascha until the feast of the Mother of God in August. The voiceless theologians the-ologize, the beautiful rocks and all of creation, each with its own voice or with its voicelessness. If you reach out your hand to a little plant, it immediately shouts loudly with its natural fragrance,

"Ah! Can't you see me? You hit me!" Everything here has a voice and, with the blowing of the wind, as they are moved, they join together in a harmonious musical doxology towards God.

When the monk cleans the senses in stillness, the mind becomes peaceful and the heart is cleansed, and he receives grace and the light of knowledge. He becomes completely light, completely mind, completely transparent. Then he gushes theology, such that even if three people were to write down his experiences they wouldn't manage, the flow of waves is so great, and it spreads peace and the complete cessation of the passions throughout the body. The heart is enflamed from love of God and shouts out, "slow down the waves of Your grace, my Jesus, for I am melting like a candle!" And truly he melts without suffering. The mind is taken up into divine vision; and a mixing takes place. Man is transformed and becomes one with God, such that he doesn't recognize himself, just as iron becomes one with fire.[8]

Through knowledge of himself the Christian becomes wiser than other people. At the same time, he develops humility and receives grace from the Lord.

[8] This should not be misinterpreted as a pantheistic confusion of the divine and human. Elder Joseph's words at the end of the sentence give us the proper interpretive framework to understand, within the bounds of Christian theology, his experience. The image of iron in the fire was used during the Christological controversies of the fourth through sixth centuries to show how, while there is a real union between the two natures of Christ, there is no confusion between them. In this particular case, however, Elder Joseph is not using the image in relation to Christology, but in relation to the distinction (defended by St. Gregory Palamas) between the Essence and Energies of God. The same analogy, however, is applicable in this case: while there is a real union between God and man through His uncreated Energies, there is not a confusion between the two—man does not participate in the Essence of God, which is completely different than man and beyond man. For a more thorough

Neglect plots against us. It's like a drought that hinders any kind of planting. It hurts everyone. It hinders those who want to begin the spiritual battle and stops those who have begun it. It hinders those who are unaware and keeps those who have been deluded from returning.

Whatever we don't give to God for Him to use, the other will use. For this reason our Lord gave us the commandment to love with all our heart and soul, so that the evil one won't be able to find a place of rest within us.

When grace works in the soul of one who is praying, the love of God floods the soul to such an extent that he is unable to handle his experience. Afterwards his love turns toward the world and mankind, which he loves so much that he asks to take upon himself all human suffering and grief so as to free those who suffer. And more generally, he identifies with every grief and affliction, even of irrational beasts, so that he weeps when he considers their suffering. These are the attributes of love which prayer energizes and inspires. For this reason those who are dedicated to prayer never cease interceding on behalf of the world. As strange and as bold as it may seem to say, the prolongation of the life [of this world] is due to these people. Know that if such people cease to exist the end of the world will come.

When you want to learn the will of God, abandon your own will completely along with every other thought or plan and with much humility ask God in prayer for His understanding. And so, whatever you feel sketched or laid on your heart, do it and it will be according to God's will. Those who have even more presence and candor in seeking God's will hear within themselves more clearly the answer, become more careful in their lives, and

treatment of the subject, see Dr. Georgios Mantzaridis's *The Deification of Man*. Crestwood, NY: St. Vladimir's Seminary Press, 1984.

don't do anything without divine guidance.[9]

W hen someone whom you know judges you and tempts you is present, it is almost impossible for him not to bother you, as much as you may try to remain unaffected. After pardoning and praying for him, however, you recover from the grief of sadness.

[9] This counsel should not be associated with the tendency in the West to emotionalize and psychologize Christian faith. Many people look for a "good feeling" as a sign that they are on the right path. Unfortunately, this good feeling is usually the result, not of the rejection of one's will and openness to the will of God, but rather of our getting our way, when our mind consents to our will. The process Elder Joseph is referring to is much more profound and requires a real ascetic effort to deny one's own will and to truly seek God's will, with tears and pain of heart. Elder Joseph's words are reminiscent of Archimandrite Sophrony's words in *St. Silouan the Athonite*, where the issue is dealt with in depth (77-84). Fr. Sophrony, while affirming the truth of Elder Joseph's words, explains that,

"The man who adopts this course will succeed only after he has learned by experience how the grace of the Holy Spirit operates; and when fierce self-denial has taken root in his heart—that is, if he has resolutely determined to deny his own petty individual will in order to acquire and fulfil the holy divine will." However, Fr. Sophrony goes on to explain that, "most people neither hear nor understand God speaking in their hearts: they listen to the urging of passion, which inhabits the soul and with its clamour drowns the still small voice of God. In the Church another course lies open to us—to seek out and obey the counsels of a spiritual father. This is what the Staretz [St. Silouan] himself did, considering the humble path of obedience to be the most trustworthy of all." (78-79). In the same way, as Dr. Constantine Cavarnos writes, Elder Joseph "emphasizes that, generally, a spiritual striver needs a wise and experienced guide, in order to tread safely and successfully the path that leads to purity and spiritual perfection." *Prolegomena* to *Monastic Wisdom: The Letters of Elder Joseph the Hesychast.* Florence, AZ: St. Anthony's Greek Monastery, 2000 (32).

The beginning of the path toward pure prayer is the battle against the passions. It is impossible to progress in prayer as long as the passions still exist. In spite of this, the presence of the grace of prayer is not blocked as long as one is not careless or proud.

You don't see how, with every prayer you utter, many demons fall and turn back. You only see how much you are wounded. Know that they, also, are being beaten, and flee. Each time we show patience they flee in leaps, and with each prayer they are seriously wounded. So, in the time of war, don't expect that while you are firing bullets and cannonballs that they'll retaliate with Turkish Delight and chocolates!

Active love without submission cannot exist. How can you love and serve if you don't first submit to the other's will? Every movement of active love is service, and so those who obey serve in two ways. On the one hand they show their faith in the one giving the order, and on the other hand they show their love through the service rendered.

If someone wanted to live with me, he would hear my prayers and sighs and would see the tears I shed for all my brethren. All night I pray and shout, "Lord, save all my brethren, or else blot me out as well! I don't want Paradise if I'm on my own!"

Elder Paisios the Athonite

5

ELDER PAISIOS

On July 25, 1924 the future Elder Paisios (Eznepidis) was born to pious parents in the town of Farasa, Cappadocia in Asia Minor. The family's spiritual father, the priest-monk Arsenios (the now-canonized St. Arsenios of Cappadocia), baptized the babe with his name, prophesying his future profession as monk. A week after the baptism (and barely a month after his birth), Arsenios was driven, along with his family, out of Asia Minor by the Turks. St. Arsenios guided his flock along their 400-mile trek to Greece. After a number of stops along the way, Arsenios's family finally ended up in the town of Konitsa in Epiros (in northwestern Greece). St. Arsenios reposed, as he had prophesied, forty days after their establishment in Greece, and he left as his spiritual heir the infant Arsenios.

The young Arsenios was wholly given over to God and spent his free time in the silence of nature, where he would pray for hours on end. Having completed his elementary education, he learned the trade of carpentry. He worked as a carpenter until his mandatory military service. He served in the Army during the dangerous days of the end of World War II. Arsenios was brave and self-sacrificing, always desiring to put his own life at risk so as to spare his brother. He was particularly concerned about his fellow soldiers who had left wives and children to serve.

Having completed his obligation to his country, Arsenios

received his discharge in 1949 and greatly desired to begin his monastic life on the Holy Mountain. Before being able to settle there, however, he had to fulfil his responsibility to his family to look after his sisters, who were as yet unmarried. Having provided for his sisters' future, he was free to begin his monastic vocation with a clean conscience. He arrived on Mt. Athos in 1950, when he learned his first lessons in the monastic way from the virtuous ascetic Fr. Kyril (the future abbot of Koutloumousiou Monastery), but was unable to stay by his side as he had hoped, and so was sent to the Monastery of Esphigmenou. He was a novice there for four years, after which he was tonsured a monk in 1954 with the name Averkios. He was a conscientious monk, finding ways to both complete his obediences (which required contact with others) and to preserve his silence, so as to progress in the art of prayer. He was always selfless in helping his brethren, unwilling to rest while others worked (though he may have already completed his own obediences), as he loved his brothers greatly and without distinction. In addition to his ascetic struggles and the common life in the monastery, he was spiritually enriched through the reading of soul-profiting books. In particular, he read the lives of the Saints, the *Gerontikon*,[1] and especially the *Ascetical Homilies* of St. Isaac the Syrian.

Soon after his tonsure, monk Averkios left Esphigmenou and joined the (then) idiorhythmic brotherhood of Philotheou Monastery, where his uncle was a monk. He put himself under obedience to the virtuous Elder Symeon, who gave him the *Small Schema* in 1956, with the new name Paisios. Fr. Paisios dwelt deeply on the thought that his own spiritual failures and lack of love were the cause of his neighbor's shortcomings, as well as of the world's ills. He harshly accused himself, pushing himself to greater self-denial and more fervent prayer for his soul and for the whole world. Furthermore, he cultivated the habit

[1] Gerontikon (*The Sayings of the Desert Fathers*): The collected sayings of the Ascetic Fathers of the fourth-century Egyptian desert.

of always seeking the "good reason" for a potentially scandalous event and for people's actions, and in this way he preserved himself from judging others. For example, pilgrims to Mt. Athos had been scandalized by the strange behavior and stories told by a certain monk, and, when they met Elder Paisios, they asked him what was wrong with the monk. He warned them not to judge others, and that this monk was actually virtuous and was simply pretending to be a fool when visitors would come, so as to preserve his silence.

The Elder with a young pilgrim

In 1958 Elder Paisios was asked to spend some time in and around his home village so as to support the faithful against the proselytism of Protestant groups. He greatly encouraged the faithful there, helping many people. Afterwards, in 1962, he left to visit Sinai where he stayed for two years. During this time he became beloved of the Bedouins, who benefited both spiritually as well as materially from his presence. The Elder used the money he received from the sale of his carved wooden handicraft to buy them food.

On his return to Mt. Athos in 1964 Elder Paisios took up residence at the Skete of Iviron before moving to Katounakia, at the southernmost tip of Mt. Athos, for a short stay in the desert there. The Elder's failing health may have been part of the reason for his departure from the desert. In 1966, he was operated on and had part of his lungs removed. It was during this time of hospitalization that his long friendship with the then- young sisterhood of St. John the Theologian in Souroti, just outside of Thessaloniki, began. During his operation he greatly needed blood and a group of novices from the monastery donated blood to save him. Elder Paisios was most grateful, and after his recovery did whatever he could, materially and spiritually, to help them build their monastery.

In 1968 he spent time at the Monastery of Stavronikita helping with both its spiritual and material renovation. While there he had the blessing of being in contact with the ascetic Elder Tychon who lived in the hermitage of the Holy Cross, near Stavronikita. Elder Paisios stayed by his side until his repose, serving him selflessly as his disciple. It was during this time that Elder Tychon clothed Fr. Paisios in the *Great Schema*. According to the wishes of the Elder, Fr. Paisios remained in his hermitage after his repose. He stayed there until 1979, when he moved on to his final home on the Holy Mountain, the hermitage Panagouda, which belongs to the Monastery of Koutloumousiou.

It was here at Panagouda that Elder Paisios's fame as a God-bearing elder grew, drawing to him the sick and suffering people of God. He received them all day long, dedicating the night to God in prayer, vigil, and spiritual struggle. His regime of prayer and asceticism left him with only two or three hours each night for rest. The self-abandon with which he served God and his fellow man, his strictness with himself, the austerity of his regime, and his sensitive nature made him increasingly prone to sickness.

In addition to respiratory problems, in his later days he suffered from a serious hernia that made life very painful. When he was forced to leave the Holy Mountain for various reasons (often due to his illnesses), he would receive pilgrims for hours on end at the women's monastery at Souroti, and the physical effort which this entailed in his weakened state caused him such pain that he would turn pale. He bore his suffering with much grace, however, confident that, as God knows what is best for us, it could not be otherwise. He would say that God is greatly touched when someone who is in great suffering does not complain, but rather uses his energy to pray for others.

In addition to his other illnesses he suffered from hemorrhaging, which left him very weak. In his final weeks before leaving the Holy Mountain, he would often fall unconscious. On October 5, 1993, the Elder left his beloved Holy Mountain for the last time. Though he had planned on being off the mountain for just a few days, while in Thessaloniki he was diagnosed with cancer that needed immediate treatment. After the operation he spent some time recovering in the hospital and was then transferred to the monastery at Souroti. Despite his critical state he received people, listening to their sorrows and counseling them.

After his operation, Elder Paisios had his heart set on returning to Mt. Athos. His attempts to do so, however, were hindered by his failing health. His last days were full of suffering, but also of the joy of the martyrs. On July 11, 1994, he received Holy Communion for the last time; and the next day, Elder Paisios gave his soul into God's keeping. He was buried, according to his wishes, at the Monastery of St. John the Theologian in Souroti.

Elder Paisios, perhaps more than any other contemporary elder, has captured the minds and hearts of the Greek people. Many books of his counsels have been published, and the monastery at Souroti has undertaken a great work, organizing the Elder's writings and counsels into impressive volumes befitting his memory. Thousands of pilgrims visit his tomb each year, so as to receive his blessing.

Elder Paisios on his way to church

COUNSELS

The humble are like nightingales that hide in ravines and spread joy to the souls of men with their sweet songs.

We mustn't despair when we struggle and continuously see nothing but the slightest progress. We all do nearly nothing, some a little more, some a little less. When Christ sees our little effort He gives us an analogous token and so our nearly nothing becomes valuable and we can see a little progress. For this reason we mustn't despair, but hope in God.

Unfortunately, in our days, there are many people who upset the mother Church. Of these, those that are educated have understood dogma with their minds and not with the spirit of the Holy Fathers. At the same time, those who are unlettered have grabbed hold of dogma with their teeth, which is why they grind their teeth when they speak about ecclesiastical topics. In this way, greater harm is caused by those in the Church than by those who battle it from without.

That which is asked of every Orthodox person is to instill a "good uneasiness" into the heterodox,[2] that they might understand that

---

[2] Heterodox: That is, those who hold dogmas that the Church deems erroneous.

they are in delusion. This is so they will not falsely calm their conscience and thus be deprived in this life of the rich blessings of Orthodoxy and in the life to come of the even greater and eternal blessings of God.

The person who is possessed by material things is always subjugated to unhappiness and anxiety: he trembles for fear, on the one hand that his things will be taken away from him, and on the other, that his soul be taken from him. Now, the miser whose hand is sore from his tight hold his possessions had also squeezed his own heart, turning it into stone. In order for him to be healed, he must visit unhappy people, to suffer, so that slowly, slowly, he is forced to open his hand and his heart of stone will start to soften. It will become a human heart, and in this way the gates of Paradise will also open.

When a monk doesn't find spiritual work, he cannot be helped even by his elder, and spends his time with external things. He becomes spiritually wild and, even if he were to be tied down in his cell, he could not sit still. He will always enjoy contact with people, to give tours, to speak about the domes and archeology [of the monastery], to show them the pots with various flowers, to treat them to rich, worldly meals, and to give rest only to worldly people.

The monk flees far from the world, not because he detests the world, but because he loves the world and in this way he is better able to help the world through his prayer, in things that don't happen humanly but only through divine intervention. In this way God saves the world.

The monk is helped greatly when the monastery is far from the world, far from archeological sites and worldly noises. Even monasteries that are great sites of pilgrimage lose sight of their true goal, for many times from being a monastery they end up as a business. For this reason some bishops, very rightly, would like to have these sites, for monastics must love poverty, which they were ordered by God to preserve. Unfortunately, however, they do not limit themselves to the necessary, the simple—as much for themselves as, more generally, for the monastery. Nor do they refuse things from the faithful, or encourage them to help, on their own, our poor, suffering brethren. What do they do instead? They gather the sweat even of the poor and fill the monastery with a huge amount of oil lamps and bells, thinking that God is glorified in this way. This type of piety, however, is like the piety which many Russian clerics had, who became the cause, without intending it, of the oil lamps, chandeliers, and bells being made into cannons so as to hit the very Church of Christ.

When an elder doesn't have much experience, but has a great deal of love and much humility, he is able to help his spiritual children by means of the guidance of more experienced elders, as well as by the grace of God, which he continually receives due to his great humility.[3] However, the young cleric who gathers young people as his disciples reveals his great pride, which he has down to the marrow of his bones. He is like a baby born with a beard—a monster—and those that follow him reveal that they have an ailment of the brain or heart. Also, those clerics who study psychology so as to help souls using human contrivances are not spiritually well. The strange thing is that their teachers of psychology don't believe in God or in the existence of the soul. If they accept the soul's existence, they do so in their own unique way. In this way these clerics show that they are spiritually sick

[3] This is an exception to the use of the word "elder" (and the first time this usage has arisen in this text). It is occasionally used in Greek in this general sense. The word is used metaphorically in this case, to indicate the wisdom of the cleric or monastic in choosing the path of service to the Church, regardless of whether he is old or young.

and that they need to be examined by the Holy Fathers. Having been healed, they would be able to discern, on their own, the sick spirit and would experience divine grace at the same time. Thus from that time forth they would use the divine energy for those suffering souls and not human contrivances.

Those who rush to be made spiritual fathers, though they still have many spiritual toxins, are like unripe, sour quince, which, as much sugar as we may pour on, never becomes a nice sweet; but, even if it does, it quickly gets sour.[4] Sweet words and great truths have value when they come from genuine mouths, and are received only by those souls that are well-disposed and by those great people who have a pure mind.

One word of a humble and [spiritually] experienced man that is painfully born from the depths of his heart has greater worth than a bunch of clever sayings of an external man[5] that come out quickly from his educated mouth. His words don't speak truth to the souls of men, for they are fleshly words and not the flames of the fire of Pentecost.

If a passionate man[6] tries to correct an egotist, steel hits flint and fires are ignited! If he tries to correct a sensitive person, he hurts him greatly. It would be like a wild man taking a thick wire brush to clean out a little mucus from a baby's eye.

[4] In Greece not all priests are given the blessing by their bishop to hear confession and to receive the faithful as spiritual children. This is a charismatic ministry that is given to those priests able to fulfill its grave responsibilities.

[5] External man: Not so much an extroverted man as a man whose life revolves around the things of this world, whose internal world is undeveloped and unexplored.

[6] Passionate man: Not so much a man with a fiery temper as a man who is under the influence of his passions (among which are gluttony, lasciviousness, slothfulness, listlessness, and so on, in addition to anger).

What a wonderful thing it will be when we know ourselves! Then humility will be for us a state of being, and God will position us well with His divine gifts. Then the spiritual laws will cease working, and the one who rises the highest will humble himself, for we will all walk low, we won't fall, and we will continually receive the grace of God which is given to the humble.

Holy asceticism together with its great self-denial, which is born from great faith in a burst of love for God, brings man to true joy. He is happy to live, for his heart flutters, glorifying his God of benefactions. He is also happy to die, for he thus goes close to God again, and will continue there his doxology.

Virtue has the habit of betraying man, wherever he may hide. Though he may act as a fool-for-Christ,[7] still he will be betrayed, though it may be later on, and he will help many souls.

The goal of reading is the application, in our lives, of what we read. Not to learn it by heart, but to take it to heart. Not to practice using our tongues, but to be able to receive the tongues of fire and to live the mysteries of God. If one studies a great deal in order to acquire knowledge and to teach others, without living the things he teaches, he does no more than fill his head with hot air. At most he will manage to ascend to the moon using machines. The goal of the Christian is to rise to God without machines.

Let us not expect the spiritual spring if we don't first pass through

[7] Fool-for-Christ: A spiritually advanced person who takes on the extreme asceticism of foolishness (apparent madness) for Christ's sake. It is the ultimate rejection of the ways of the world, refusing even normal contact with the world, so as to detach oneself wholly from it. It is an unusual calling and only for a very few. Often part of the fool-for-Christ's service to the world is that of a prophet calling the world to repentance.

the spiritual winter during which the spiritual vermin die. We mustn't expect the divine to blossom within us if the human hasn't first died.

Costly [fervent] love, which sacrifices itself and does not partake of the world, is itself consumed by the love of God from within. The life of man is then a continuous Lent and all of his days are a continuous joy of light. Costly love for God, with its sacrifices, sweetens the heart to boiling, and divine love, which cannot be held in, like steam, soars and so unites to God. This state of spiritual madness not only takes man out of himself, but even the heart is taken from the flesh, that is, from the fleshly desires, and is clothed completely in, and refined in, God.

Those who constantly partake of the love of God are often indifferent to material nourishment. Or, if they eat, they don't taste the food, for even then they continue to feel God intensely and to partake of the sweet blessing of His love. When the heart becomes a furnace through the love of God, it is then able to burn up all vanity that approaches, and this brings internal peace when man passes through the fiery trials of his life.

There are no people more blessed than those who have made contact with the "heavenly television station" and who are piously connected to God. In the same way, no people are more wretched than those who have cut contact with God and wander, dizzy, around the world, flipping through the world's many television stations so as to forget, if only for a short time, the anguish of the derailment of their lives.

It is very helpful to read a bit of the *Gerontikon* before beginning to pray. Then your heart will warm up, the lid will come down on your many worldly cares, and you will be able to pray without distraction.

In the hour of prayer, when our mind wanders to thoughts of bad things, or if these thoughts come without our wanting them, we shouldn't wage an offensive war against the enemy; because, even if all the lawyers in the world joined together, they wouldn't make any headway with a little demon. Only through ignoring these thoughts can one chase them away. The same is true for blasphemous thoughts.

If you want to grab God's attention so He'll hear you during prayer, turn the dial to humility, for God always works in this frequency; then humbly ask for His mercy.

My brother, don't ask for anything in prayer except for repentance. Repentance will bring you humility, humility will bring you the grace of God, and God will uphold you in His grace and will give you whatever you need for your own salvation, as well as whatever is needed, should the case arise, for you to help another soul in need.

When man is spiritually healthy and distances himself from other people, so as to better help them through his prayers, then he regards all people as holy and only himself does he regard as a sinner.

If we haven't got control of our mind during the hour of spiritual study we are not benefited at all. We simply yawn and tire ourselves without a goal, for we cannot remember anything. In the same way, when the printer doesn't have his mind on his work and forgets to put ink in, the printing presses work without printing anything.

All evil begins in the mind, when it is interested only in science. Scientists don't find their inner peace and their balance then. However, when their minds are attached to God, scientists use their science to cultivate their inner world and to help the world, for their minds are sanctified.

The mind, when it begins to spend time near God, oftentimes forgets, not only its dwelling, but even this dwelling of the soul, this earthen flesh.

In all things we must put forth good thoughts and refuse to accept evil telegrams,[8] if we want to purify our heart and change the evil machines of the heart into good machines; then gold will be turned into holy chalices and broken bells into chandeliers.[9] Even discarded paper will be turned into fresh napkins. However, when the heart is evil and views good gold as bronze, it will make it into bullets and cannonballs.

Oh, blessed desert—by which created man is so greatly helped to be reconciled with his Creator, and is transformed into an earthly Paradise—as you gather once again the wild animals around the person you tamed!

As much as is possible, love the desert and the immaterial life, and fly from your material possessions to the fold of the poor. Simplify your life so as to be freed from worldly anxiety, so that your life might have meaning.

Conscience is the first law of God, which He carved deeply into the hearts of the first-created. In turn we each make a photocopy from our parents when we're born. Those who manage to heighten their sense of conscience through daily study of themselves feel themselves to be foreigners in this world, and worldly people are baffled by their gracious behavior. Those

[8] That is, bad thoughts.

[9] The Greek word Elder Paisios uses is *polielaios*, which refers to the special chandeliers found in many Orthodox churches.

Elder Paisios with his prayer rope

who haven't studied their conscience benefit neither from their spiritual studies nor from counsels from their elders. They won't even be able to keep God's commandments, for they have lost their senses altogether.

The soft life makes people useless. Without toil and struggle sanctification doesn't come.

[When one realizes one's sinfulness and the great mercy of God,] the heart cracks, as hard as it may be, and real tears fall of themselves and then man prays and weeps without effort. This is because humility works continuously together with *philotimo*[10] and drills on the heart so that the springs increase, and the hand of God continually strokes the hard-working and *philotimo* child.

Let us struggle with all our powers to gain Paradise. The gate is very narrow, and don't listen to those who say that everyone will be saved. This is a trap of satan so that we won't struggle.

Christ is wholly love, goodness and consolation, and never suffocates. He has an abundance of spiritual oxygen.

[God allows temptations] so as to dust off our soul, for it to be purified through sorrows and weeping, so that we are forced to take refuge in God for our salvation.

Theology is the word of God that is comprehended by pure, humble, and spiritually reborn souls. It is not the beautiful words of the mind which are formed with philological artistry and which are expressed with the juridical or worldly spirit. Created words can't speak to man's soul, just as a beautiful statue is not able to speak, unless the audience is very worldly and is satisfied

[10] *Philotimo*: A word Elder Paisios was fond of using, for which there is no equivalent in English. According to Elder Paisios's understanding, *philotimo* "is the reverent distillation of goodness, the love shown by humble people, from which every trace of self has been filtered out. Their hearts are full of gratitude towards God and to their fellow men, and out of spiritual sensitivity, they try to repay the slightest good which others do them." Elder Paisios the Athonite, *Epistles*. Souroti, Greece: Holy Monastery of the Evangelist John the Theologian, 2002, 34.

Elder Paisios

simply by beautiful words. Theology that is taught as a [worldly] science usually examines things historically and consequently understands things externally. Because patristic asceticism and inner experience are absent, this theology is full of doubts and questions. With his mind man is not able to comprehend the divine energies unless he first struggles ascetically to live these energies, so that the grace of God might work within him.

Children contract their first spiritual colds from the open windows of their parents' senses. The mother passes on her cold especially when she is not modestly dressed and scandalizes her children with her behavior.

The holy life of parents instructs the souls of their children and so they naturally obey them and grow up with piety and without psychological problems, and the children are pleased with their parents. The parents are gladdened by their children in this life and in life eternal, where they will once again glory in them.

Whoever is at peace in the material world and is not concerned about the salvation of his soul is like the senseless birds who don't make a noise from within the egg, so as to break the shell and come out to enjoy the sun—the heavenly flight in the life of Paradise—but instead remain unmoving and die inside the egg shell.

The pretense of worldly politeness is very harmful, for it fools one and opens one's heart to the worldly person, and in the final analysis it wastes one's piety, for the worldly person doesn't know what piety is. It's like giving golden pounds to people that only know bronze pennies.

Blows are necessary for the salvation of our souls, for they cleanse the soul. The more one hits and rubs clothing, the better it is cleaned. Similarly, the more one hits octopus and cuttlefish, the more they are softened and washed from ink.

Live in constant glorification of and thanksgiving towards God, for the greatest sin is ingratitude and the worst sinner is the ungrateful person.

At the beginning of the spiritual life, out of love, God doesn't allow anyone to realize either his sinfulness or the many benefactions that He bestows on him, so as to keep him from despair, especially if he is sensitive.

Those who are in the world must not despair when they are overcome by many passions, and when their nature is unruly and races passionately downwards. Rather, they must trust in the almighty power of God and turn the steering wheel of their powerful engine back onto the road toward God, upwards. Soon after they will pass other, slow-moving cars, which for years have been driving the road toward God.

Elder Philotheos of Paros, with an icon of his onetime spiritual
guide, St. Nektarios of Pentapolis,
in the background

6

ELDER PHILOTHEOS

Blessed Elder Philotheos (Zervakos) was born in May 1884 in the small village of Pakia in the Peloponnese. His devout parents, Panagiotis and Katerina, gave him the name Konstantinos in baptism. From an early age, Konstantinos was very pious and was constantly in church. He relates an account in his autobiography that illustrates his acute sense of the spiritual world as a young boy: "When I was about eight or ten years old...the devil appeared in front of me in old ripped clothes and shoes, with a terrible face and horns on his head. He stood about 25 or 30 feet from me and began throwing stones; they fell to either side of me but didn't hit me."

After Konstantinos completed his public school education, his parents sent him to a special school for the training of teachers. He graduated at the age of 17 and became a teacher. Initially he hoped to go to America to teach in one of the schools that were being established by Greek parishes there. As it turned out, God had other plans for him. Soon afterwards, on reading the lives of Sts. Barbara, John of Damascus, and Anthony the Great, among others, he felt a divine sweetness, which enflamed his heart with love for God and divine things. Throughout the day his mind clung to the memory of God and of Heaven and, through the lives that he had read, he experienced the sufferings of the martyrs and the sweet silence of the desert monastics. This led him to desire the monastic life. Having revealed his desire to his mother, the same night he was visited by demons in the form of grotesque monsters, which threatened to kill him if he didn't give up his desire to pursue the monastic life. Gripped with fear, Konstantinos called upon the Theotokos to come to his aid. Suddenly her icon descended from the heavens and the demons were driven away. When the icon began to ascend, the demons returned, angrier than before. This happened three times. The third time, Konstantinos clung to the icon until he came to himself and stayed awake, trembling until the morning.

From that time on Konstantinos feared being outside after dark, and the initial calling he felt to the monastic life waned. Although the things of the world tempted him, God did not abandon him and protected him despite his change of heart. He soon took a teaching position in the nearby village of Phoinikion. In addition to his work, he spent time playing the violin, mandolin, and guitar, and would recite poetry in the marketplace at the request of the villagers, who gave him the nickname "nightingale," as his voice was so beautiful. One day, at a friend's house, his eyes happened upon a beautifully bound book entitled *Diamonds of Paradise*, a compilation of lives of Saints, and other spiritually edifying writings. Konstantinos, his heart aflame once again with love for God, took the book and went straight home to read it. Touched once more by grace, he decided to give up the things of the world—his music, acquaintances with worldly people, and all other things that bound him to the earth. The thought of his death and how his soul would fare at the Final Judgement especially moved him.

Konstantinos continued to teach and had a significant effect on the tender hearts of his pupils. In his words, "I managed to implant so much faith and fear of God into their hearts that one would think that those children weren't children, but angels of God!" Because of the new path his life was taking and the positive influence he had on others, the demons returned and began tormenting him once again. His autobiography is full of graphic descriptions of his battles with them. After one such battle, he recounts, "I realized I was in a place where wicked spirits dwelt. I saw a large number of unclean demons working and pounding, as if in a workshop, constructing various traps for catching people." He finally overcame his fear of the dark and of the attacks of the demons, with the thought that God, who cared for him during the day, would certainly not abandon him at night. With increased faith and boldness, he began to visit by night the deserted chapels in the Greek countryside, praying while the world slept. Every time he was assailed by demons, in various forms, he would call on the Theotokos and she would come to his rescue.

Increasingly, Konstantinos felt the calling to the monastic life. After he made a positive decision, however, his parents repeatedly hindered him, particularly his father, who threatened to commit suicide if he left. On one of his attempts to find a monastic home, he walked barefoot with nothing but his Bible and the clothes on his back. Arriving tired and bruised in Patra, he was advised by Fr. Eusebios Matthopoulos to return home to fulfill his military duty, "giving unto Caesar what is Caesar's," and waiting to "go and serve the heavenly king."

In 1905, Konstantinos moved to Athens, where he had been called by the government to do his military service. During his two and a half years of military service he was able to continue his education during the evenings, as well as to attend the sermons of Fr. Eusebios, who had by that time moved to Athens. During his stay in Athens Konstantinos had the good fortune of meeting and spending time with Alexandros Moraitidis,[1] Alexandros

Elder Philotheos

[1] Alexandros Moraitidis (1850-1929): A philologist, novelist, playwright, and journalist from the island of Skiathos. He was part of the intellectual elite at the turn of the century that remained faithful children of the Church.

Elder Philotheos: tireless confessor, apostolic-
missionary priest, and preacher of repentance

Papadiamantis,[2] St. Nicholas Planas, as well as St. Nektarios of
Pentapolis. When Konstantinos's military service ended, he
spoke with St. Nektarios about where he should go to become
a monk. St. Nektarios told him the following: "Your goal is
good, but I advise you to go to no other monastery than the
one at Paros, Longovarda, where the brethren are virtuous and
numerous." The twenty-three year-old Konstantinos, however,
wanting to fulfill his desire of many years, decided to head north
to Turkish-controlled Macedonia and in particular, to the Holy
Mountain of Athos. The first thing he did on arriving in Thessaloniki was to venerate the tomb of St. Demetrios, for whom

[2] Alexandros Papadiamantis (1851-1911): Greece's most important novelist
of the nineteenth century. He was also from the island of Skiathos and was
a faithful son of the Church.

he had great love and reverence. Soon after his arrival, however, the Turks suspected him of being a spy. He was condemned to death by the Pasha's secretary, but the Pasha,[3] previously unaware of Konstantinos's case and not having given his consent to his execution, rescued him and sent him back to Athens.

It was not until a number of years later that Konstantinos learned why the Pasha had saved him. A friend with whom he had traveled to Thessaloniki related to him a conversation he had had afterwards with the Pasha, who recounted that,

> One morning, as I was sleeping peacefully, St. Demetrios came into my room wearing a general's uniform and carrying his weapons. He looked at me austerely and ordered me, "Get up now! Get dressed, put your shoes on and go to such-and-such a place in the city so as to free a young man who has been unjustly condemned to death by your private secretary. When you free him, send him to the steamship 'Mikali' which is in the port and preparing to set sail for Greece." I hastened at once to save the young man from danger, and sent him to Greece.

Konstantinos repented of his disobedience and eventually made his way to the Monastery of Longovarda, where the abbot and brethren welcomed him with much love and joy. He was tonsured into the Small Schema in December of 1907, seven months after entering the monastery. He was given the name Philotheos, which means "Lover of God," and the next day he was ordained to the diaconate. A few years later, in 1910, Fr. Philotheos made a pilgrimage to the Holy Mountain with the blessing of his spiritual father. Although he made a number of soul-benefiting acquaintances there, he was generally disappointed by the spiritual state of Mount Athos. Passing through

[3] Pasha: The title of the Ottoman (Turkish) governor of any particular region.

Elder Philotheos in Egypt (1924)

Thessaloniki on his return south, Fr. Philotheos was again imprisoned by the Turks for espionage, and, once again, St. Demetrios came to his rescue.

Fr. Philotheos returned to Longovarda, and in April of 1912 he was ordained to the priesthood. In October of the following year, he was elevated to archimandrite. His elevation to archimandrite marked a change in Fr. Philotheos's life, and he began hearing confessions and preaching on the islands of the Aegean, and later in Athens, the Peloponnese, and in other parts of Greece. In March of 1924 he made an extensive trip, confessing people and preaching in southern Greece, Crete, Palestine, Arabia, Egypt, and Mt. Sinai. Fr. Philotheos was profoundly affected by his time in the Holy Lands and would later urge Christians to go on pilgrimage there, rather than going on tours of Europe.

In the same year, disorder descended upon the Church on account of the New Calendar innovation introduced in 1923 by Patriarch Meletios Metaxakis, and accepted by the Synod of the Church of Greece in 1924. The schism that the innovation caused, pitting Orthodox Christians following the original and the New Calendars against one another, greatly pained the Elder, and he prayed for the restoration of the traditional (Church) calendar and the reconciliation of the two groups. Even though the Elder did not separate himself from his bishop on account of the change, nor concelebrate with those who did, he was one of the most outspoken opponents of the innovation. Until the end of his life the Elder maintained that, even though the cause of the schism was the calendar innovation and the only path to unity was the restoration of the traditional calendar, neither group was free of fault, but both fell under different anathemas.[4] "For more than forty years I have begged and I continue to beg God to calm this awful storm, this dreadful rough sea in the Church, and to bring Her peace, and one night I heard an invisible voice say: *To the wayward, crooked paths are sent by God....*I wish and pray and entreat the Heavenly Father to enlighten the lead-

[4] He wrote, on the one hand, that the "new calendar was neither introduced into the Orthodox Church by an Oecumenical Council nor by a Local Synod. Rather, the Oecumenical Patriarch Meletios (Metaxakis), who was a thirty-three degree Mason, together with six anti-orthodox minded hierarchs, introduced it anti-canonically and illegally, thus showing contempt for the Orthodox Church and the traditions of the Holy Apostles and Holy Fathers." With regard to the Old Calendarist groups, on the other hand, who had separated from the official Church, the Elder wrote that they had likewise erred and fallen under anathema, in that they "are transgressors and scorners of the first tradition of the Great commandment of Love. The commandment of love—they disdain it, violate it, cast it out, hating one another, biting at one another, beating up on one another." He was especially upset that "certain zealot old calendarists believe and are of the mindset that the Mysteries without the calendar are invalid and that without the calendar there is no salvation. A greater heresy than this does not exist!" *Letter of Elder Philotheos to Papa-Demetri Gagastathis* (in Greek, dated January 20, 1960), found in *Πάπα-Δημήτρης Γκαγκαστάθης (1902-1975).* Thessalonica, Greece: Orthodox Kypseli Publications, 1990, 238-243 (in English: *Papa-Demetri-Gagastathis*

ers of the Church to cease attacking one another...but rather to reconcile themselves and to return the Church to the Orthodox calendar of the fathers...."[5]

When Ierotheos, the abbot of Longovarda, reposed in January of 1930, Archimandrite Philotheos was elected to take his place. Although only forty-six years old, he had already distinguished himself by his great piety, unwavering faith in God, love of labor, humility, and by his zeal for the Church's tradition, and was considered by many to be a Saint. In addition to his added responsibilities at the monastery, Fr. Philotheos continued to make missionary trips to other parts of Greece, to preach and to encourage the people of God.

During the Italian and German occupation (1941-1944), he worked tirelessly to aid the poor and starving people of Paros. Between 150 and 200 islanders would eat at the monastery daily, and it is estimated that 1500 people would have died had the monastery not been able to feed them. At one point Elder Philotheos interceded with the German commissioner of Paros for 125 innocent young Greeks condemned to death. The commissioner, unwilling to back down, finally gave in when Fr. Philotheos offered to be executed along with them.

After the war Elder Philotheos continued his missionary activities. He would go a number of times a year to various islands, as well as to many villages and cities throughout northern and southern Greece, teaching, exhorting, and hearing confessions. In addition to his position as abbot of Longovarda, he also gave spiritual direction to various women's monasteries. In his autobiography, he notes that often during these missionary journeys, "I would be so exhausted that I would fall into bed as though dead, with the thought that I would never rise again but die, or lie ill, immobile and inactive for many days....However, when I awoke in the morning, I would feel completely healed and healthy. This amazed me...and made me realize my wretchedness and weakness as well as the strength and Grace of God (without which we can do nothing)."

In addition to his gifts of confessing and preaching, Fr. Philotheos also possessed the gift of writing. In a letter to him, the writer Takis Papatsonis[6] praised him, suggesting that his "gift as a writer rivals the elegance of the works of the educated Church Fathers." Fr. Philotheos was a prolific writer. Although he managed to publish only nine complete books, he also wrote articles, pamphlets, and around 10,000 letters of spiritual direction to spiritual children around the world. The blessed Elder wrote to encourage the people of God to continue the spiritual struggle and to remain faithful to the holy tradition they had inherited from the Fathers of the Church.

Elder Philotheos continued to encourage and guide the people of God up until the time of his death. A few weeks before his repose he was visited by Archimandrite Dionysios of the Monastery of Simonopetra, one of his spiritual children. He heard Elder Philotheos's final confession, and the next day the Elder partook of Holy Communion. He reposed shortly afterwards, on the morning of May 8, 1980. In his honor, people throughout Greece wrote eulogies in praise of his many virtues. The venerable Abbot Gabriel (1886-1983) of the Monastery of Dionysiou on the Holy Mountain, wrote one of the most beautiful and moving ones:

> Twelve days ago the dean of our spiritual circles fell asleep, the teacher and guide of the mysteriological life of our country, the venerable Fr. Philotheos, the pride of monasticism....I cannot find words to speak worthily of the great preacher of repentance and the unshakeable pillar of Orthodoxy.

(1902-75). Thessalonica, Greece: Orthodox Kypseli Publications).

[5] Ibid., 242-243.

[6] Takis Papatsonis (1895-1976): An athenian poet, essayist, and academic.

Elder Philotheos, the "great preacher of repentance and
the unshakeable pillar of Orthodoxy," in his latter days

COUNSELS

The present transitory life is like the sea, and we are the ships. Just as ships at sea, we don't encounter only peace, but many times we meet with strong winds and great storms, scandals, temptations, sicknesses, sorrows, distress, persecutions, and various dangers. We mustn't lose courage, however. We must be bold, courageous, and faithful. If we lose courage in the face of dangers, as timid humans of little faith, let us call on Christ as Peter did, and He will reach out His hand and help us.

Parents must teach their children from their earliest days. They must teach them the fear of God, must cut their bad impulses and faults, and they mustn't fawn upon them or satisfy their bad desires and appetites. The small child is like the soft candle that you shape as you like and which accepts whatever seal you put on it. Whatever letters you write on a clean sheet of paper will remain imprinted. In the same way, whatever the small child learns when he is small will remain imprinted until old age....When the tree is small, if the wind blows, it bends. If we put a pole next to it, it becomes straight. If we don't put up a pole, and it remains bent, it will always remain bent. If, when it has grown up and is well rooted, we want to straighten it, it breaks and is cut down. It is the same way with our children. Let us support them in the faith and in the fear of God when they are small. Let us fence them in and surround them with walls of instruction and good examples until they get rooted in virtue, when they won't fear any danger.

People today are unrestrained. Laity and clergy, like unbridled horses, run to sin. They don't take into account God, death, the Judgement, repayment—nothing...nothing. They are only interested in the material world, in the body, in pleasures, in honors. There are very few who are truly interested, and perhaps for these few God spares the world.

Christians are divided into two groups, those that are lettered and those that are unlettered. Most unlettered people are non-believers. They don't know that God exists, what God is, and what faith is. They do, however, learn all sorts of myths, and so many immodest songs and dances! Most lettered people are completely non-believing and, except for a few exceptions,...they never pray, and are ashamed to make the sign of the Cross.

In order for the nation to be straightened out, evil habits and sin must cease.

The path of life you follow, married or unmarried, is the will of God. For, many times, people desire one thing, while the call of God is otherwise. The married state is good, as is the unmarried; the celibate state is better and higher, for the unmarried man is interested in how to please God, while the married man thinks of how to please his wife and the world. God doesn't force any-one, either into the married or into the unmarried state. On his own, man must choose one path or the other. If one hesitates as to which of the two paths to follow, let him pray fervently, with compunction and piety, that God might reveal it to him.

In this present evil generation, the spiritual father must use Economy—for, if he implements exactness, none or only a few of those coming to confession would be found worthy of receiving Holy Communion. The greatest care and discernment is necessary, however, and the spiritual father must pray fervently to the Heavenly God and Father to enlighten him as to how to implement Economy.

He who is obedient is an imitator of Christ, and he who is proud and talks back is an imitator of the devil....So-called Christians must be true, [Christians] in word and deed, and not false, [Christians] only in name.

The easiest, quickest, and safest path to Heaven is humility. This is the only safe path.

I am proud of the cassock I wear and consider it more valuable and seemly than every other kind of garment, even than the royal purple robes of kings. I consider myself unworthy to dress in such a modest, honorable and holy garb, which was honored by numberless monastic Saints, monk-martyrs, confessors, and Saints.[7] I am saddened by and pity those clerics who reject the cassock and who shave their beards.

Faith guides man to fear. To fear of what? To fear of sin, to fear of saddening God. The fearful person is humbled. And he who is humble has the Holy Spirit within him.

True happiness is not the honors and pleasures of the body. True happiness is virtue. As many as fight to acquire virtue, to put into practice the commandments of God, these are the truly happy.

[7] Elder Philotheos uses the Greek words *osioi*, which we translate as "monastic Saints," and *osiomartyres*, which we translate as "monk-martyrs."

Some people don't partake of Holy Communion at all due to impiety and an absence of faith. Others, out of ignorance, weakness of faith, carelessness, and an absence of true and pure love for God, partake one or two times a year as a habit, without fear, faith, and love. It is sad and worthy of great lamentation for the priest to stand at the Beautiful Gate[8]and invite Christians to commune, and for not one person to come forward.

Deep feeling, the grinding and mourning of the heart, sighing, prayers, fasts, vigils, and tears are indications of true repentance. This is genuine and true repentance. This repentance is beneficial, for it bears remission of sins for the sinner and makes him the friend of God.

The reason [why we don't all become Saints] is within us. Firstly, due to our bad intent. Secondly, due to our neglect and laziness. Thirdly, due to the lack or complete absence of love for God and the things of Heaven. Fourthly, due to our complete love of money, our devotion to material things, and our low-mindedness.

When the enemy tempts you with thoughts of faithlessness, with all your heart say, "I believe completely whatever the Church believes, whatever Christ says in the Holy Gospels, whatever the Holy Apostles and Holy Fathers said. I don't, however, believe you, devil, for you are a liar and a thief."

If a man builds a house and leaves it without a roof, this house can't be used at all. In the same way, if a man acquires all the

[8] Beautiful Gate: Translation from the Greek, *Oraia Pili*, which refers to the central entrance (of the icon screen) to the altar area in an Orthodox church. It is an ancient term that was inherited from the Old Testament. One of the entrances in Solomon's temple was known by this name. In English it is sometimes referred to as the "Royal Doors."

Elder Philotheos wrote thousands of letters
to his spiritual children and to inquirers

virtues but not love, the house remains roofless and is of no benefit at all.

Let us live in imitation of all the Saints and have them always as aids and protectors. Let us imitate their struggles and virtues, especially humility, faith, hope, and love.

The meek person is stripped of sin, for God dwells in the meek. The one who has been cleansed shines with the rays of the Holy Spirit and acquires love.

When I read the lives of the Saints as a child, I felt as though a ray of divine light had entered my heart. It filled my heart with sweetness, joy, and jubilation and lit a desire and love for God and heavenly things.

Elder Porphyrios

ELDER PORPHYRIOS

The blessed Elder Porphyrios was born on February 7, 1906 in the small village of St. John Karystia on the island of Evia. His poor but pious parents Leonidas and Eleni gave this, the fourth of their five children, the name Evangelos in baptism. Little Evangelos worked hard tending the animals on his parents' farm from an early age and even went to work in a local coal mine so as to earn extra money for his family. The local school was poorly run and didn't offer much to the village children. Thus, Evangelos only received the equivalent of two years of schooling.

When he was still very young, his devout father taught him the Supplicatory Canon to the Mother of God and catechized him as best he could. Little Evangelos was drawn to the Church, Her services and especially to the monastic life. While tending his flock on a mountainside, he read the life of St. John the Hut-dweller. His heart became aflame with love for St. John and for the monastic life. Thus he decided to follow the Saint's example, and attempted a number of times to go to become a monk on the Holy Mountain of Athos. His initial attempts were foiled for various reasons, but he eventually managed to make it there at the tender age of fourteen.

By the providence of God the young Evangelos met a virtuous priest-monk on the boat to the Holy Mountain who took him under his care and introduced him to the monastic way of life.

There, in the hermitage of St. George, in the Skete of Kavso-kalyvia at the southern tip of Mt. Athos, Evangelos dedicated himself to strict asceticism and prayer. The only complaint he had of his elders, Fr. Panteleimon and his half-brother Fr. Ioannikios, was that they weren't strict enough with him. He would walk barefoot along the rocky and snowy paths of Mt. Athos, and would sleep in snatches on the hard floor of his cell, covered with just a thin blanket. He made many prostrations throughout the night, removing the clothing from his upper body so as to keep from falling asleep. In addition to his strict asceticism, he also worked hard, cutting down trees and carrying heavy sacks of soil so as to plant a garden on the rocky slopes of Kavsokalyvia. Soon after his arrival, the elders of the hermitage, seeing Evangelos's enthusiasm and the seriousness of his calling, tonsured him a monk with the name Nikitas.

The young monk Nikitas managed to continue his education through the monastic "university" of the daily cycle of services. He learned the Church's prayers, services, and hymns, as well as the Gospel readings, by heart and repeated them while he worked. Before long Nikitas was visited for the first time by an abundance of divine grace. His experience of divine grace changed his whole person: body, mind, soul, and spirit. Having been found a humble and worthy dwelling place of the Holy Spirit, the monk Nikitas was blessed with supernatural gifts. He found that, through the grace of the Holy Spirit, he could see prayers that had been offered in the past, the human soul, good and evil spirits, and many other things. He spoke with all of creation, understanding the language of animals and birds. From ancient rocks he learned about the spiritual struggles of ascetics who had lived near them. He was able to look at people, diagnose their sicknesses and heal them. From the first sign of these spiritual gifts monk Nikitas carefully obeyed Fr. Panteleimon's admonition to be cautious and to keep knowledge of his gift to himself. He used his gifts for the benefit of his brethren and those who came to see him, never being so bold, however, as to benefit himself.

Unfortunately, monk Nikitas, worn down by strict asceticism, became seriously ill with pleurisy and was forced to leave the Holy Mountain so as to recover from his sickness. He spent some time at a monastery on the mainland and then returned to Mt. Athos. The sickness returned, however, and at the age of nineteen, he was forced to leave his beloved Holy Mountain and to continue his monastic vocation at the Monastery of St. Charalambos on the island of Evia. Soon afterwards Archbishop Porphyrios III of Sinai, while visiting the monastery, recognized Nikitas' many gifts and his maturity, and decided to ordain him deacon and then priest. Thus, at the young age of twenty-one, the monk Nikitas was ordained to the priesthood with the name Porphyrios. The bishop in charge of the monastery, Metropolitan Panteleimon of Karystia, took part in the ordination and soon after gave the newly ordained Porphyrios the assignment of serving the Church as a spiritual father and confessor. Elder Porphyrios quickly received the reputation of being a God-bearing elder, a gifted knower of souls, and thus people flocked to him for guidance. He was tireless in his service, seeing people all day and occasionally throughout the night as well.

Elder Porphyrios's life took a number of unexpected turns and, after serving at a few villages of Evia, he found himself serving at the chapel of St. Gerasimos in the Polyclinic of Athens, not far from Omonoia Square. Arriving in October of 1940, he served as the Polyclinic's chaplain for thirty years, in addition to continuing his service to the thousands of faithful who flocked to him for confession and guidance. He was given a tiny stipend by the Polyclinic, but in order to survive he was forced to create various other sources of income. He was given use of the small Monastery of St. Nicholas on the edge of Athens and worked hard to build a garden and repair the buildings, with the hope of eventually housing a monastery for women there.

Elder Porphyrios was troubled by many sicknesses throughout his life: kidney problems, a hernia, a heart attack, stomach hemorrhaging, and eventually blindness. Many times the doctors gave up hope of his recovery, but he would get well and continue his tireless work. Near the end of his life he began working especially hard to lay the foundations of the women's monastery that he had hoped to build for a number of his spiritual daughters who wanted to live the monastic life. When it became clear that it would not be possible to establish it on the site of the Monastery of St. Nicholas, he began to look elsewhere. For years he traveled, visiting hundreds of possible sites until, in the late 1970's, he found the most appropriate location in Milesi, Attica, about an hour's drive from Athens. He managed to have the foundation of the monastery church laid just a few years before his repose.

Throughout his life, but especially near the end, Elder Porphyrios felt increasingly drawn back to the place of his monastic repentance—the hermitage of St. George, Kavsokalyvia on the Holy Mountain. He managed to have some of his monastic spiritual children take up residence in the empty buildings there, and thus secured the spot of his final repose. About six months before his repose Elder Porphyrios left the world to return to the Holy Mountain. He spent his final days in prayer and repentance, though he was forced twice to return to Attica during this period so as to help his spiritual children. In the early morning of December 2, 1991, Elder Porphyrios reposed, his monastic brothers having kept vigil with him throughout the night.

Elder Porphyrios was greatly troubled throughout his lifetime by individuals who claimed to speak for him and to represent his opinions, using his name to support their positions. Although he believed strongly about certain ecclesiastical issues, he generally kept his thoughts to himself, revealing them to a few select people when the occasion arose and when it was necessary. He was a true "son of the Church," and remained in humble obedience to Her. He knew experientially that bishops are bearers of divine grace. He would also say that it is better that one make mistakes within the Church, than to be "correct" but outside of it. Elder

Elder Porphyrios with sisters of the monastery

Porphyrios taught that Christ's greatest desire was for the unity of the faithful, for each member of the Orthodox Church to identify with the struggle and pain of his brother, to carry one another's burden and to live our lives as though we are one body. For this reason, as he reposed he repeated over and over again Christ's words from Gethsemane, from His prayer to His Heavenly Father, "That they all may be one; as thou, Father, art in me, and I in thee, that they also may be one in us: that the world may believe that thou hast sent me" (John 17:21).

Elder Porphyrios

COUNSELS

Life without Christ is not life. That's the way it is....If you don't see Christ in everything you do, you are without Christ.

Christ is our Friend, our Brother; He is whatever is beautiful and good. He is everything. In Christ there is no gloom, melancholy or introversion, whereas man suffers from various temptations and situations that make him suffer. Christ is joy, life, light, the true light, which makes man glad, makes him fly, makes him see all things, see all people, suffer for all people, and want all people to be with him, close to him.

It's possible for people to come to the point of despair and see before them the living reality of chaos and say, "We're falling into chaos! Everyone get back, get back, go back, we've been deceived," and thus return to the path which leads them to God, and for our Orthodox Faith to shine. God works in mysterious ways and doesn't want to influence man's freedom. He arranges things so that slowly, slowly, man goes where he is supposed to.

Every person who insults us, wrongs us, slanders us, who wrongs us in any way, is a brother who fell into the hands of the worker of evil, the devil. When we challenge this brother we must feel great sorrow for him, sympathize with him, and beseech God fervently and quietly to strengthen us during the difficult hour of our trial and to have mercy on our brother who became a victim of the devil. God will help us as well as him.

When our brother errs we must bear his temptation. True love inspires us to make sacrifices for the good of our neighbor. Without sacrifice and with our condemnation, we cause our brother who fell to fall even further; while, with the silent sacrifice of our love and prayer for him, we awaken his conscience, which awakens and condemns him, and so he repents and is corrected.

True Christians, in the souls of whom Christ lives, are unable to do anything else except love all people, even enemies. The crown of our love for our friends has elements that are out of place (calculation, reciprocity, vanity, emotional weakness, passionate sympathy),[1] while the crown of love for our enemies is pure.

Our love in Christ must reach all places, even to the hippies in Matala [in Crete]. I very much wanted to go there, not to preach to them or to condemn them, but to live with them, without sin of course, and leave the love of Christ to speak of itself, which transfigures life.

Only the religion of Christ unites and we must all pray that people come to this. Thus union will not occur by believing... that religions are the same. They are not the same....Our Orthodoxy is not related to other religions.

In order for others to love you, first you must love.

The martyrs suffered greatly when they were tormented. They suffered in the same way as any normal person would have suffered, with the difference that they were continually united to

[1] Passionate sympathy: With the sense of the ascetic term "passion." Thus, the Elder is referring to sympathy that has an element of self-love and selfishness.

Christ through prayer and partook of a force which was greater than their pain, and in this way they were able to conquer. If, however, they had abandoned prayer, even for just a moment, their pains would have become unbearable and they would have been ready to deny Christ. However, hanging onto prayer, they were strengthened and endured the pain of their martyrdom until the end.

When we're in the grace of the Holy Spirit our prayer becomes pure. Let us pray continuously, even while lying on our bed, while we're preparing for bed, or while we're resting.

There is an electric generator and in the room is a lamp. If, however, we don't flip the switch, we will remain in darkness. Similarly, there is Christ and there is our soul. If, however, we don't flip the switch of prayer, our soul will not see the light of Christ and will remain in the darkness of the devil.

Do you know what a great gift it is that God gave us the right to speak to Him every hour and moment, wherever we are? He always listens to us. This is the greatest honor we have. For this reason we must love God.

When you pray, make prostrations even if this tires you. Prayer that is accompanied by voluntary sacrifice becomes more pleasing to God and is more effective.

When you pray for someone who is suffering from sinful passions under the influence of the devil, don't tell the person that you're praying for him. Otherwise the devil will learn about it and will influence his soul to rise up against you and so your prayer will have no effect. Pray for the person secretly and your prayer will be effectual.

You are unable to be saved alone, if all others are not also saved. It is a mistake for one to pray only for oneself, for one's own salvation. We must pray for the entire world, so that not one is lost.

I am not afraid of hell and I do not think about Paradise. I only ask God to have mercy on the entire world as well as on me.

A bad book does you harm. A good book is good for you. Even if you aren't ready to put into practice what you read, because you have the desire inside of you, slowly, slowly, in time, without violence and pressure, the desire for the good matures and finally you put it into practice.

[Read the Gospel,] for it truly contains a treasure and solves all problems. It is true philosophy. It is philosophy derived from revelation, the truths of God as they have been preserved since the beginning. There are no other truths.

We must acquire the grace of God as quickly as possible. Without the grace of God our attempts will not bear fruit and we won't go to Paradise. God gives us His grace when we are humble.

What is the spiritual battle? Well, the soul is a garden divided into two parts. On one half are planted thorny bushes, and on the other half, flowers. We also have a water pump with two taps and two channels. The one guides the water to the thorns and the other to the flowers. I always have the choice to open one or the other tap. I leave the thorns without water and they dry up, I water the flowers and they blossom.

When Christ comes and dwells throughout the soul, then all problems disappear along with all delusions and worries; then sin departs as well.

Be especially careful of and don't understimate the demon of listlessness.[2] When it subjugates the soul it drugs and paralyzes it. It is a large demon and enters man together with a great number of other demons.

We must not approach Christ out of fear of how we will die and of what will become of us. Rather, we must open our hearts to Him, as when we tug at a curtain and the sun immediately shines in. In this way Christ will come to us, that we might truly love Him. This is the best way.

Whatever we do, let us do it because we want to, freely, responsibly and with gladness.

Read a lot so that God might enlighten your mind. You know what? I would read a lot. In fact, I would climb up a tree with a ladder I had fashioned and would pull it up with me as I ascended, so that people wouldn't see me and bother me. I spent hours there in study.

You find yourself in a darkened room and you move your hands so as to try to brush away the darkness which, of course, doesn't move. If you open a window and light enters, the darkness disappears. The same happens with study. The Holy Scripture, the lives of the Saints, and the writings of the Fathers are the light that chases away the darkness of the soul.

Continue along your path. The devil will come with his tempting thoughts and will tug at your sleeve, so as to disorient you. Don't turn to him, don't start a conversation with him, and don't oppose him. In this way the devil will get bored and will leave you alone.

[2] *Akydia*: An ascetic term derived from the Greek verb *kidevo*, which means, "to tend," "to take care of." When preceded by the negative prefix, "a-" the word suggests one's negligence and absence of care, and generally denotes a spiritual state of listlessness.

We know when the Holy Spirit visits us. We don't doubt it at all. It's not like one of our normal feelings. It is something that comes from above and transforms us completely, making us into different people. When Christ comes within us, then we live only the good; we live love for the entire world. Evil, sin, and hatred disappear on their own; they can't remain, there is no place for them.

Every person who has sin within him is very confused. He must leave open a crack in his soul so that the light and love of Christ might enter in. Thus he will begin to disentangle his soul. The initiative always belongs to Christ. Man must accept it and then with his own watchful effort he will be able to sense the greatness of the things God is revealing to him.

You aren't able to repent properly and to be alone in the heights of love of God. That is to say, [just] God and you, Christ and you. The love of Christ is offered and always passes through other people.

Confession is a way for man to come to God. It is the offering of the love of God to man. Nothing and no one is able to deprive man of this love.

The melancholy person revolves around and is interested only in himself. The sinner who repents and confesses comes out of himself. The confessor and the spiritual father are wonderful aspects of our faith. So confess to your elder what you need to, and receive remission of your sins, then don't look back.

Occasionally we should also make a general confession, as different psychological wounds and various events leave us with psychical sicknesses. During confession we shouldn't limit ourselves only to the confession of our sins but we should also include the various tempting thoughts such as fear, sadness, joy, and annoyance which are provoked in us by events such as

Elder Porphyrios

earthquakes, deaths, marriages, lack of faith, and so on.

I beseech those who have known me to pray for me, for I also, in much humility, prayed for you. However, now that I leave for Heaven I have the sense that God will tell me, "What do you want here?" I have one thing to say to Him, "I am not worthy, Lord, to be here, but may Your love do as it will with me." From that point on I don't know what will happen to me. My wish, however, is that God's love will operate.

Obedience leads to humility, humility to discernment, discernment to vision, vision to clairvoyance.[3]

[3] The word Elder Porphyrios uses is *pro-orasi*, an ascetic term that refers to a special charisma given by God to those humble souls who will use it to

Let us be humble, but not pretend to be humble. Pretension to humility is a trap of the devil, which brings despair and inertia, while true humility brings hope and the fulfilling of the commandments of Christ.

If a person is to change, the grace of God must come, but in order for the grace of God to come, man must be humbled.

The Christian needs to avoid sickly spirituality, as much the feeling of superiority for one's virtue as the feeling of inferiority for one's sinfulness. To have a complex is one thing, to be humble is quite another. Melancholy is one thing, repentance something else.

Souls are tortured by the passions and they rest near the love of God.

Because I didn't have much experience when I first began [hearing confessions], I would give heavy canons[4] to monks and laymen who came for confession. Many of them, after a short period, would come to me again and would tell me that they weren't able to keep these canons. Now I realize how heavy the canons I would give were—this was due to my inexperience.

the glory of God and for the upbuilding of the Church, and not for selfish or prideful ends. This spiritual gift takes various forms enabling the person who has it to see into the souls and minds of people, to see future events, as well as to see distant events as though they were nearby. As mentioned in the biography of Elder Porphyrios, he was a bearer of this charisma. In his words, "The Holy God, in order to help me do His work better and to bring more people close to Him, has given me the charisma of seeing a bit more than others see." Great spiritual discernment is necessary, however, as we know from the experience of the Church that the evil one is able to imitate spiritual gifts (though only superficially) so as to fool people and lead them astray.

[4] Canon: In this case, a special rule of prayer, fasting, etc. given to the repentant to aid him in his return to God.

When I became a monk I felt better. Even my health improved. Although previously I had been sickly, afterwards I became healthier, with the ability to bear labors with psychical courage. Above all, however, I felt eternal. The Church is a mystery. Whoever enters the Church doesn't die, he is saved, is eternal. Thus I always feel eternal, as though immortal. Having become a monk, I believe that death does not exist. This thought captivates me.

Orthodox asceticism is not just for the monasteries, but also for the world.

Our sicknesses do us well when we endure them ungrudgingly, ask God to forgive our sins, and glorify His name.

It is possible for happiness to exist [in marriage], but with one presupposition: the spouses must have acquired spiritual wealth, loving God and keeping His commandments. In this way they will end up truly loving one another and will be happy. Otherwise they will be psychically poor, they won't be able to give love, and they will have demonic problems that will make them unhappy.

A bad wife may be your opportunity to make it to Paradise.

Don't pressure your children. In your prayers say the things that you want to tell them. Children don't listen through their ears, but only when divine grace comes to enlighten them do they listen to the things we want to tell them. When you want to say something to your children, tell it to the Panagia and she will bring it to pass. This prayer of yours will be like a spiritual caress which will embrace your children and will grab their attention. Sometimes we try to caress them and they react against it, but they never react against the spiritual caress.

Parents who have difficult and bad-mannered children shouldn't try to deal with them, but with the one who is behind their children, the devil. We can't fight the devil until we become Saints.

You mustn't wage your Christian struggle with sermons and arguments, but with true secret love. When we argue, others react. When we love people, they are moved and we win them over. When we love we think that we offer something to others, but in reality we are the first to benefit.

Whether we go to Paradise or to hell doesn't depend on if we have a lot of or a little money, but on the way we use the money we have. Money, possessions, and all material goods are not our own, but God's. We are simply responsible for the way in which they will be used. We must know that God will ask an account from us for every last cent, whether or not we used it according to His will.

The false witnesses of Jehovah are unfortunate and may God have mercy on them. They irritate some Christians; others quarrel with them and call them names, while others take them to court. But Chiliasm[5] cannot be fought in this way. Only when we become holy will it be fought.

[5] Chiliasm: Also known as "millennialism," and refers to an ancient heresy which teaches that Christ's Second Coming will be followed by a period of a thousand years during which Christ will rule on earth. The Jehovah's Witnesses along with many Protestant groups adhere to this teaching, which is a misinterpretation of the enigmatic book of *Revelation*. Chiliasm is a dangerous heresy as it teaches people an erroneous view of the End Times and thus will make them more vulnerable to the deceits of the evil one during the final period of history. For more on the Orthodox understanding of the End Times, see Elder Cleopa's *The Truth of Our Faith*, 193-213, or Dennis Engleman's *Ultimate Things*. Ben Lomond, CA: Conciliar Press.

Today people want to be loved and for this reason they are unsuccessful. The correct way is to not be interested in whether or not people love you, but whether or not you love Christ and people. This is the only way that the soul is fulfilled.

[When asked how one should vote, the Elder responded in parable:] The Orthodox Church is like a brooding hen. Under Her wings she covers black chicks and white chicks, yellow chicks, and chicks of every different color.

Psychiatrists and psychologists are like blind men who, with the sense of touch, attempt to understand the things around them. The soul is very deep and only God knows it.

What can politicians do for you? They are confused by their psychical passions. When a person is unable to help himself, how can he help others?

When I abstain from food I am better able to understand the soul of man.

If I make a mess of things with the bishop, if the bishop is upset with me, my prayer doesn't rise to Heaven.

The truth is in Orthodoxy. I have lived it and I know it by the grace of God. There are many lights which man sees and which make an impression on him, but only one is the true light.

Don't pass these things I tell you on to other people—my words are the appropriate medicine for you, for your particular situation. The same words spoken to someone else, though externally he may seem to have the same symptoms as you, won't produce the same beneficial results.

Elder George of Drama

8

ELDER GEORGE

The blessed Elder George (Karslidis) was born in Argyroupolis, Pontos in 1901. His faithful parents Sava and Sophia baptized this their second son with the name Athanasios. They died when he was still very young, and so it was his pious grandmother who raised him, instilling in him a holy fear of God and a fervent love for the Church's divine services.

Athanasios's birthplace, Pontos, is a place with a great spiritual heritage from the earliest years of Christianity. Great Fathers of the Church, such as the three Great Hierarchs, Sts. Basil the Great, Gregory the Theologian, and John Chrysostom, spent a good amount of time there, struggling in the ascetic life. In addition to its rich history of asceticism, it also has a rich history of martyrdom, the most recent addition being the sufferings of the Christians under the Turkish yoke.

In such a difficult period of persecution, the young Athanasios was particularly fortunate to live in Argyroupolis, which is in one of the few regions of Pontos that managed to preserve a certain amount of freedom. There, under the positive influence of the important monastery of Panagia Soumela, in addition to two others, Peristereota and St. John Vazelonos, the Christians managed to raise and educate their young people in the faith and culture of their ancestors.

At the tender age of five Athanasios began tending the family's flocks. With patience and love he bore the harsh treatment of his older brother who made life difficult for both Athanasios as well as for his younger sister Anna. Although painful, the loss of their parents and their brother's mistreatment of them bore spiritual fruit, for they wisely accepted these trials with love and faith in God. When Anna died at a young age, light emanated from her grave, drawing villagers to the cemetery. When her remains were exhumed three years later her bones were found to have the same beautiful yellow color of the relics of those the Church has glorified as Saints. Thus, Athanasios's early days were permeated both with the piety and holiness of lives dedicated to God, as well as with the pain of the corruption and instability of this life. This very realistic understanding of life was to prove to be a firm foundation for Athanasios's future spiritual development.

The situation at home having become increasingly difficult, Athanasios, at the age of seven, decided to run away. One winter's day, with his few possessions in a bag, he left home. God, of course, did not abandon him, but saved him from various perils and led him to a family of crypto-Christians.[1] They cared for him and loved him as a son, a love that increased when the father of the family had a dream in which a noble man informed him that Athanasios would bring many souls to God.

One day St. George, who would protect Athanasios, and care for him throughout his life, appeared to him and told him to mount his horse. With the aid of St. George, Athanasios traveled to Tiflis, Georgia, where a pious priest cared for him. The priest, amazed at the young boy's spiritual maturity and gifts, clothed him in the cassock which, from the age of nine, he would never abandon. Soon afterwards he began his monastic life at a Georgian monastery where, though much younger than the other brethren, he matured quickly in the spiritual life. He patiently waited nearly ten years to be officially tonsured a monk, which took place in July of 1919. He was given the new name Symeon.

[1] Crypto-Christians: Christians, who, like the earliest Christians, practice their faith secretly, so as to escape the persecution of the anti-Christian state.

During his tonsure the bells of the monastery began to ring of their own accord, yet another sign of divine providence for this soul which had suffered and which would suffer so much.

The continuation of the young Symeon's sufferings were not slow in coming, as his monastery was soon closed by the communists. The monks were incarcerated in a wretched dungeon-like prison. At one point Symeon was taken out of the prison, stripped, and with his hands tied behind his back was paraded through the streets as the people mocked him. He was returned to prison where he awaited his martyrdom.

The imprisoned monks and clergy asked permission at Pascha to go to church. Having been denied this, they fervently prayed for continued strength in their struggle. As they chanted, "Christ is risen,"[2] the prison shook and the doors opened of their own accord. The inhabitants of that area hastened to see what was happening and beheld three holy figures who, chanting "Lord have mercy" and holding a cross, were processing in a circle above the prison. The vision lasted until dawn, when the captives were prepared for execution. They were tied together and led to the edge of a cliff. The firing squad took aim and fired. Three bullets hit Symeon, but they only grazed him, and did little harm. He was dragged off the cliff, however, by the weight of the others. Miraculously, he fell without being killed and thus escaped death.

He was soon imprisoned again, but was eventually released through the efforts of the pious wife of a Russian. He was tended to by devout Christians, and on his recovery was ordained priest, in October of 1925, by Metropolitan John Tsiaparaski of Grouzia Scheta, and given the new name George. By this time he had acquired the reputation of being a God-bearing elder, and so people flocked to him.

Although his life continued to take many unexpected turns, he always remained faithful to the life of prayer and pious spiritual

---

[2] The traditional Orthodox hymn of Pascha.

Elder George as a young priest-monk
before his departure from Georgia

struggle he had learnt as a child. This remained the basic fabric
of his life, despite the various external conditions that were forced
upon him. The Elder was very strict with himself throughout his
life, eating mostly wild greens and sleeping very little. He was
ever faithful to monastic poverty, to the extent that even when
his cassock had basically disintegrated, he gratefully declined a
friend's offer to make him a new one.

He was also fully dedicated to his new responsibilities as a
priest. He would rise at midnight to pray and prepare for the

celebration of the Divine Liturgy. He served the liturgy with great attention, slowly and with care that the proper spirit be cultivated and preserved. During the preparation of the elements, God would inform him of the spiritual state of those he commemorated, both the living and the dead. With great pastoral discernment he would pass the information on to his parishioners, either to encourage them to pray more fervently for the souls of the deceased or to bring sinners to repentance. Before bringing the Holy Communion out to the faithful, he would ask that those who wanted to commune come to the left-hand door of the iconostasis[3]where he would read the prayer of absolution over them and anoint them with oil. Like other contemporary elders and many Saints throughout Christian history, Elder George would sometimes be seen levitating during the Divine Liturgy. While he celebrated he would often be visited by the Saints, who would serve with him. There are countless accounts by parishioners of the Saints who made their presence felt while Elder George served.

In 1929, with the help of close friends, Elder George managed to go to Greece. Although we cannot be certain of his reasons for going, we may hypothesize that one reason was his failing health which, because of his continuous imprisonment and persecutions, had deteriorated a great deal. Not yet thirty years of age, he was already extremely weak and semi-paralyzed—he had essentially lost the use of his legs. After passing through many difficulties on his arrival in Greece, he finally managed to settle in the village of Sipsa (now Taxiarches) near Drama in northern Greece. Despite his terrible physical condition, many of the pious faithful recognized the sanctity and virtuous life of Elder George and were drawn to him as to a source of water in the desert. Various families in the village, through whose care and herbal remedies his legs were partially healed, took him in.

In 1936 the Elder managed to make a pilgrimage to the Holy

---

[3] Iconostasis: The icon screen at the front of an Orthodox church.

Lands. While there, in addition to venerating the sites of Christ's life and sufferings, he also visited various monasteries and hermitages. In a hermitage near the Monastery of St. Sava, God miraculously informed a hermit that the monk (Elder George) passing by was his nephew. With great joy they embraced and the Elder asked his uncle for guidance, whether he should stay in the world to serve the people or escape to the monastic solitude of the Holy Mountain. His uncle counseled him to remain in the world, to serve the world that had fallen into such spiritual darkness. On his return from the Holy Lands the Elder joyously recounted the events of his pilgrimage.

He continued to be housed by the pious villagers until 1938, when the Greek government made a permanent distribution of farmland. The Elder was given an acre of land, on which he managed, always with the help of the villagers, to build the foundations of a humble monastery dedicated to Christ's Ascension. The monastery was officially consecrated in 1939.

Most of the accounts of Elder George's biography come from this second stage of his life, during his pastoral work among the people of Sipsa and, more generally, in the region around Drama. There are many, many accounts of his spiritual gifts that he used for the spiritual and material benefit of those who came to him. Here we will relate just a few of the more instructive ones.

Among the many people who flocked to the Elder were some that had been to see psychics and mediums. Having the gift of spiritual discernment, he realized their sin and refused to receive them, knowing that they viewed him as just another "medium." When he realized that those coming would be open to correction, he gently but adamantly insisted on their rejection of the counsels of demons.

The Elder foresaw the coming of World War II to Greece and wept especially heavy tears the week before war was declared. He also foresaw the civil war that would follow the Second World War, warning his spiritual children at the end of the war, "Don't

Elder George as a young priest-monk

rejoice, don't rejoice, the things coming now are worse...."
During the civil war, the rebels came to destroy the village of
Sipsa and to kill its inhabitants. Their leader repented, however,
saying, "They are poor people, why should we harm them?"
When they returned to their headquarters, the other rebels were
upset and another group went to destroy the village. They had
the same experience of repentance, as did a third group that

went. As it became clear later on, the Elder had foreseen the coming danger and had instructed the villagers to take an icon of the Panagia in procession around Sipsa, beseeching God for the protection of the village. The villagers had heeded his word, and in this way the village was saved.

Many years after the war, in 1958, a man visited the Elder. He had just bought a lottery ticket and as he traveled to the monastery he thought about what he would buy if he won the lottery. As soon as he arrived, the Elder told him, "You have a lottery ticket in your pocket. Throw it away and never buy lottery tickets again. I won't allow you to buy the things that you have in mind to buy, should you win. Also, don't buy the plot of land you thought of buying in Thessalonica, but remain in your village."

On another occasion a woman visited him and before she even managed to greet him he told her, "Your hands are on fire. They are burning, but we don't see the fire. What work do you do?" She told him that she was a midwife. "How many children have you killed?" he then asked. She denied having killed any. "Shall I tell you? Five." He went on to tell her in which villages and of which mothers the children were whom she had aborted. Speechless, the lady wept and through active repentance was reconciled to God.

One day a lady brought some quinces to the Elder. A pregnant woman stopped her along the way and asked for some, but she refused. When she arrived at the monastery and gave them to the Elder, he told her, "On the way the gate of Paradise opened and you closed it."

The Elder, as a faithful disciple of Christ, was not only dedicated to prayerful intercession on behalf of the people, but also to caring for their material needs. He would do all he could to provide for those in need. Beyond giving out money, packages of food, clothing, and so on, the Elder would also buy material and sew rugs, sweaters, and socks for those in need. During the Second World War, when food was scarce and hunger widespread, the Elder would help prepare food in large pots, which he would send to the hungry inmates of the local prison. When pilgrims came to the monastery, he would care for them as a mother cares for her children, providing for their material needs first, before caring for them spiritually. He would often prepare food ahead of time and, because of his spiritual gift of foresight, the quantities were always correct.

In early 1959 the blessed Elder began to prophesy his upcoming repose. He prepared his spiritual children, strengthening them for the trials and struggles they would undergo before their final repose. To a nun who was his spiritual daughter he counseled, "Although you will suffer, act nicely towards people. They will steal from you and will slander you; they will accuse you and you will suffer many other things...Don't ask anyone for a reason, only pray for them and keep vigil, for God to forgive them."

As the day of his repose approached, he gave specific directions for his burial and informed his spiritual children of the day and time he would depart. On the eve of his repose he asked to be helped to go into the monastery church. There he venerated the icons and partook of the Holy Mysteries one last time. Returning to his cell, he made the final preparations for his departure. That night, a few hours after midnight on November 4, 1959, the blessed Elder George made his departure for his heavenly homeland. News of the Elder's death spread quickly and many people hurried to pay their last respects to their benefactor, from whose hands they had received so much good.

Although the Elder had become greatly beloved of the local people and was regarded by many as a righteous man of God, no one came to live the monastic life with him. Thus, after his repose, the monastery he had worked so hard to establish fell into disrepair until 1970, when Metropolitan Dionysios of Drama undertook its renovation. Since that time the monastic life has been re-established, with a monastic sisterhood dedicated to Christ, their monastic calling, and to the blessed memory of the monastery's founder, Elder George.

Elder George of Drama

COUNSELS

Love all your fellow men, even your enemies. This is the most basic thing. Always love not only those who love us, but also those who hate us. Let us forgive them and love them all even if they have done us the greatest evil; then we are truly children of God. Then our own sins are also forgiven...Always preach love. This is the most basic law of God: love and love alone.

Neither should wealth impress you, nor honor, but always walk justly. Eat your bread with your honorable sweat and not through unjust means. The things you gain honorably, do not squander aimlessly. Live honorably and humbly, and as much as possible extend your hands in charity...Knock on the doors of the poor, the sick, the orphans. You should prefer the homes of the afflicted to the homes of the joyous. If you do good works, you will have a great reward from God.

Why do you go to church every day, and yet you haven't made up with your children?

Continue to walk the path you are walking. Do not think that the cassock and holy garb save a person. No, first come the good works of God, humility, obedience, love, charity.

Strive to intensify your faith, and during the Divine Liturgy be undistracted and attached to the celebration of the service so that you might be granted to behold the majesties of God.

Promises to God must not be broken. God will give more.

Fasting, vigils, and prayer are heavenly gifts. However, works are also necessary, the protection and help of the poor.

Do not sit during the Divine Liturgy. Your mind should not shoot here and there. As long as you are in church, make the commitment and dedicate the whole time to prayer.

The world has abandoned innocence and goodness. Every day it takes care to head toward evil. The more years pass it heads [increasingly] toward catastrophe and God doesn't want this.

The Panagia doesn't want big candles; she wants charity given to the poor.

I must depart. It is the will of God and I must leave. Sin has progressed a great deal. The world rolls in the mire of sin and doesn't know it. And this tires me. I must depart. What makes me sad, though, are the trees[4] I planted in the garden, for they are still small and weak. They haven't had time to mature, to become trees with strong trunks, and so with the first puff of wind they will bend.

I gathered a flock of sheep and am the shepherd and take care that my sheep are as I would like them to be. When, however, I depart, my flock will be scattered. There will, of course, remain sheep in my fold, but many will sway here and there. Foreign

[4] That is, his spiritual children, whom he had struggled to raise to spiritual maturity.

sheep will also come into my fold and will learn from the faithful sheep and will not yield in any way.

N ever be jealous of wealth. Always live modestly and humbly, without egotism. Egotism is a terrible sin. When you hear someone being accused, even though it may be true, never add more accusations, but always say something positive and be sorry for the person. Take care to always love the poor, the elderly, the orphans, the sick. Spend time with poor people and with those whom others humble. Earn your living with the honest sweat of your brow. Don't forget to give alms. This is the path you must tread. Always think of what good thing you will do. These are the things that make up the life of a Christian.

T here will come a time when you will approach a tree and you won't be able to eat its fruit.

I f you pray without giving alms, your prayer is dead. Your hand should always be open. Give alms to orphans and widows. Alms and prayer go together.

T he Christian who loves all people has a great reward, especially if he forgives those who do him evil. For if we don't love our neighbor, all the good works we do will be worthless. They amount to nothing, we will be worthless. Love, my brethren, God requires love from us.

D on't be sad, for we will all depart from here. We are passing travelers. We came here to show our works and to leave.

GLOSSARY

Akathist: A service of similar size and use as the Supplicatory Canon, it is traditionally read halfway through the service of Small Compline.

Akydia: An ascetic term derived from the Greek verb *kidevo*, which means, "to tend," "to take care of." When preceded by the negative prefix, "a-" the word suggests one's negligence and absence of care, and generally denotes a spiritual state of listlessness.

Ancestral Sin: The term which best describes the fall of Adam and its anthropological implications according to the Orthodox understanding. The question of ancestral sin arises in the text in connection with the manifestations of grace in the elders as young children. Such manifestations of grace in infants are not uncommon in the lives of the Saints. These manifestations help explain how the Orthodox Church developed its understanding of man and the fall, which differs considerably from the theological position of western Christianity. Bishop Kallistos (Ware) explains the difference as follows,

> Most Orthodox theologians reject the idea of "original guilt," put forward by Augustine and still accepted (albeit in a mitigated form) by the Roman Catholic Church. Men (Orthodox

usually teach) automatically inherit Adam's corruption and mortality, but not his guilt: they are only guilty in so far as by their own free choice they imitate Adam. Many western Christians believe that whatever a man does in his fallen and unredeemed state, since it is tainted by original guilt, cannot possibly be pleasing to God....And Orthodox have never held (as Augustine and many others in the west have done) that unbaptized babies, because tainted with original guilt, are consigned by the just God to the everlasting flames of Hell. The Orthodox picture of fallen humanity is far less sombre than the Augustinian or Calvinist view.

But although Orthodox maintain that man after the fall still possessed free will and was still capable of good actions, yet they certainly agree with the west in believing that man's sin had set up between him and God a barrier, which man by his own efforts could never break down. [Timothy Ware, *The Orthodox Church.* London, England: Penguin Books, 1983, 229-230].

As becomes clear from Bishop Kallistos's exposition, the manifestation of grace in infants is a serious theological problem for many western Christians, but is wholly consonant with the Orthodox understanding. In addition to the testimony of the Saints and of contemporary elders, the careful reader of Holy Scripture will also find numerous accounts that testify to the spiritual perception of infants. One example is that of St. John the Baptist. Scripture tells us that Mary visited John's mother and, "when Elisabeth heard the salutation of Mary, the babe leaped in her womb," which Elizabeth interprets a bit further down, "lo, as soon as the voice of thy [Mary's] salutation sounded in mine ears, the babe leaped in my womb for joy" (Luke 1:41, 44). Given the Orthodox understanding of man, it is clear that this perception becomes dull later on in life, due both to man's increasingly sinful state, as well as to his increasing dependence on his rational faculty, which makes him increasingly suspicious of spiritual manifestations. Christ's words, "Verily I say unto you, Except ye be converted, and become as little children, ye shall not enter into the kingdom of heaven," (Matthew 18:3) support this view. The seminal work in English on this important theological topic is Fr. John S. Romanides's *The Ancestral Sin.* Ridgewood, NJ: Zephyr Publishing, 2002.

Antidoron: From the Greek word that means literally, "in place of the gifts." In English it is also called "blessed bread," and is given out to the faithful at the end of the liturgy. Orthodox Christians refrain from taking *antidoron* if they have not abstained from food completely from the night before.

Archimandrite: In Greek it means literally, "the head of the fold," and refers to the abbot of a monastery. In contemporary usage, it is also a title bestowed upon a celibate priest.

Asceticism: Man's struggle to keep Christ's commandments. It is the Christian's method of growing in the spiritual life which involves his bodily and spiritual effort. It is a necessary tool in one's struggle for sanctification. The insistence on remaining faithful to one's ascetic struggle in the face of bodily pain is a common theme throughout the lives of the Saints as well as in the lives of contemporary elders. Many people are quick to point to unhealthy excesses found in Medieval ascetic practices, and thus reject asceticism outright as an illegitimate aspect of Christian life. Others take refuge in psychological explanations of this phenomenon, which are inevitably mistaken, as the phenomenon is not psychological, but deeply spiritual, and has to do with man's intimate relationship with God. It is an important topic, especially as many people, living completely according to the logic of this world, refuse to accept this voluntary struggle as beneficial and glorifying to God. The discerning reader, however, will find countless references to extreme asceticism throughout Holy Scripture, in the lives of the Prophets, the Apostles, St. John the Baptist, and even of Christ Himself. One such reference are Christ's words in St. Matthew's Gospel, "Verily I say unto you, Among them that are born of women there hath not risen a greater than John the Baptist....And from the days of John the Baptist until now the kingdom of heaven suffereth violence, and the violent take it by force" (11:11-12). Theologically the question centers around one's understanding of man's role in salvation, whether it is a completely passive role, or whether there is some kind of synergy between man's will and God's will.

It is important to note, however, that the question of asceticism is a completely personal one based on the completely free relationship between man and God. There are no formulas for ascetic endeavor (although there is a generally accepted framework, as regards fasting in particular), and in the Orthodox Church each of the faithful takes counsel of one's spiritual father as to how to approach the question of asceticism. The asceticism found in these lives is unique, just as the elders whose lives are presented are unique. Critics of asceticism often base themselves on abuses of ascetic struggle that are not accurate portrayals of asceticism, but vulgar caricatures. Experienced ascetics are themselves the first to point out the dangers of asceticism, when it is undertaken pridefully, without the blessing and direction of a spiritual father, and when it is separated from the aspects of the spiritual life that it is supposed to serve (in particular the life of prayer). When considered in its proper context, however, it becomes clear that asceticism is not at all foreign to Christianity. It is, in fact, intimately related to St. Paul's teaching on the place of Christ's Cross in the life of every Christian. For a more in-depth treatment of this topic, with particular reference to Protestant misinterpretations of the New Testament, see Fr. Georges Florovsky's, "The Ascetic Ideal and the New Testament: Reflections on the Critique of the Theology of the Reformation," in *The Byzantine Ascetic and Spiritual Fathers: Volume Ten in the Collected Works of Georges Florovsky.* Belmont, MA: Notable and Academic Books, 1987.

Beautiful Gate: Translation from the Greek, *Oraia Pili*, which refers to the central entrance (of the icon screen) to the altar area in an Orthodox church. It is an ancient term that was inherited from the Old Testament. One of the entrances in Solomon's temple was known by this name. In English it is sometimes also referred to as the "Royal Doors."

Canon: (1) Regulation concerning ecclesiastical life and behavior. The Church's canonical tradition is a living tradition which, while insisting on fidelity to the historical expression and implementation of the canons, continues to develop with the Church, addressing contemporary needs and serving the spiritual goal of the salvation of souls.
(2) Ecclesiastical hymn based on the so-called "Old Testament Canticles," of Moses, of Miriam, and so on.
(3) The daily rule of prayer, reading, prostrations, and so on that the Christian keeps in his room.
(4) A special rule of prayer, fasting, etc. given to the repentant to help him along his return to God.

Cappadocian Fathers, The: Sts. Basil the Great, Gregory the Theologian, and Gregory of Nyssa. They are renowned for the depth and breadth of their secular and religious education. Their education, combined with the holiness of their lives, enabled them to serve the Church at a particularly crucial time in the explication of Christian doctrine.

Cell: From the Greek word *kelli*, it is used to refer both to the room where a monastic lives (which we render as "cell") as well as to a monastic dwelling, similar to a hermitage, housing one or more monks. In this second meaning, we render the word as "hermitage."

Chiliasm: Also known as "millennialism," and refers to an ancient heresy which teaches that Christ's Second Coming will be followed by a period of a thousand years during which Christ will rule on earth.

Concelebrator: One who serves (celebrates) the liturgy together with the main priest.

Crypto-Christians: Christians, who, like the earliest Christians, practice their faith secretly, so as to escape the persecution of the anti-Christian state.

Dependency (also known as *metochi*): Any building owned and maintained by a monastery that exists outside the property of the monastery. This includes churches, farmland, guesthouses for traveling monks, and so on.

Despotikon: The room where bishops and other dignitaries stay while visiting a monastery.

Dispassion: Not the destruction of man's senses, but their purification and transfiguration. Dispassion "is the transfiguration of the passionate aspect of the soul...rather than its mortification. Thus dispassion in this context does not signify a stoic indifference, but rather, a transfiguration and sanctification of the powers of the soul and eventually of the body also." [St. Anthony's Monastery, *Counsels from the Holy Mountain*. Florence, AZ, 1999, 423].

Economy: From the Greek word *oikonomia*, which in this case has a deep theological meaning. The Church's use of this term derives from the "Economy" of our Lord Jesus Christ, which was His great condescension, as God, to become man in the Incarnation. Though man deserved death, God reached out to man, out of love, to save him. Both the bishop and the spiritual father in the bending of certain of the Church's canons exercise Economy in the Church. According to the Fathers, Economy is to be applied as a loosening or tightening of the rule in a certain place, at a certain time, for the salvation of a certain person or persons.

Elder (in Greek, *geronda*; in Russian, *staretz*): An elder is a spiritually experienced Christian who, having himself faithfully walked Christ's path to Golgotha and experienced His resurrection, has thereby experientially learned the secrets of the way of spiritual growth. It is a charismatic ministry that is often practiced by clergy, although not by any means exclusively so.

Epitrahili: In Greek, literally, "upon the neck." It is the stole that the priest or bishop wears around his neck when hearing confession.

Fool-for-Christ: A spiritually advanced person who takes on the extreme asceticism of foolishness (apparent madness) for Christ's sake. It is the ultimate rejection of the ways of the world, refusing even normal contact with the world, so as to detach oneself wholly from it. It is an unusual calling and only for a very few. Often part of the fool-for-Christ's service to the world is that of a prophet calling the world to repentance.

Gerontikon (*The Sayings of the Desert Fathers*): The collected sayings of the Ascetic Fathers of the fourth-century Egyptian desert.

Great Entrance: The beginning of the second part of the liturgy, during which time the unconsecrated gifts are processed around the church from the holy *prothesi* to the holy altar in anticipation of their consecration.

Great Schema: The final stage of monastic profession wherein the monastic makes complete promises.

Hesychasm: A Greek word for the ascetic practice of *hesychia*.

Hesychastirion: A Greek word that denotes a place that is dedicated to the practice of *hesychia*.

Hesychia: A Greek word meaning "stillness."

Heterodox: Those who hold dogmas that the Church deems erroneous.

Holy Sepulchre: The church built over the tomb where Christ was buried.

Iconostasis: The screen that holds the icons at the front of an Orthodox Church.

Idiorhythmic: A form of monastic organization that leaves each monk to make his own program of food, work, and services. It is generally an indication of a state of decline of the monastic life.

Jesus Prayer: "Lord Jesus Christ, Son of God, have mercy upon me, a sinner," is the most basic and common prayer used by monks and laymen alike in the Orthodox Church.

Kenosis: Greek word meaning "self-emptying."

Man, External: Not so much an extroverted man as a man whose life revolves around the things of this world, whose internal world is undeveloped and unexplored.

Man, Passionate: Not so much a man with a fiery temper as a man who is under the influence of his passions (among which are gluttony, lasciviousness, slothfulness, listlessness, and so on, in addition to anger).

Menaion: From the Greek word meaning "month," it refers to the twelve liturgical books (one for each month) that include the Church's hymnographical texts for each day of the year, for the feasts and Saints' days throughout the year.

Mt. Athos (also known as the "Holy Mountain"): Mt. Athos is a monastic republic located on a peninsula in northern Greece. For over a thousand years Mt. Athos has been the most important center of Orthodox monasticism.

Mystery: From the Greek word *mysterion*. It is usually translated as "sacrament" in English, though the English word "mystery" is closer to the theological meaning of the original Greek, as it emphasizes the divine action (the "mysterious" aspect) rather than the human aspect of the Church's mysteriological ("sacramental") life.

Nepsis (adj.: neptic): A Greek word, which is translated variously as "watchfulness" or "sobriety" in the spiritual life and which expresses both of these words. Although *nepsis* and other concepts introduced in the lives and counsels may seem irrelevant to many people, they are not, however, superfluous; especially as regards the present elders—for them these concepts were very relevant and a significant aspect of their spiritual struggle.

The practical attempt to keep Christ's commandments perfectly is the proper context wherein the relevance of ascetic practices such as *nepsis* (as well as *hesychasm* and *noetic* prayer), is manifest. These are very practical means by which the ascetic attempts to perfectly keep, in particular, the first commandment, "Thou shalt love the Lord thy God with all thy heart, and with all thy soul, and with all thy mind" (Matthew 22:37). In the words of Archimandrite Sophrony,

For him [St. Silouan], the chief foundation of hesychasm was the first commandment...He writes,

The man who has come to know the love of God will say to himself, 'I have not kept this commandment. Though I pray day and night, and strive to practise every virtue, still have I failed in the commandment of love towards God. At rare moments only do I arrive at God's commandment, though at all times my soul longs to abide in it.' When irrelevant thoughts intrude into the mind, the mind is then concerned both with God and with them, and so the commandment to love God 'with *all* thy mind and *all* thy heart' is not fulfilled. But when the mind is entirely wrapped in God, to the exclusion of every other thought—that is fulfilling the first commandment, though again, not yet completely. [Archimandrite Sophrony (Sakharov), *St. Silouan the Athonite*, 142].

Neptic Fathers: Those Fathers of the Church whose writings include a practical exposition of how to train one's mind to be always attentive to the movement of thoughts that attempt to enter the mind and thereby distract it from prayer.

Noetic: A Greek word referring to man's intellect. Not to be confused with man's rational faculty, the intellect is the means by which man, in a direct manner, is able to perceive spiritual realities.

Noetic Prayer: Prayer that is characterized by the descent of the mind, saying the words of the Jesus Prayer, into the heart.

Panagia: Greek word meaning "All-Holy." It is perhaps the most popular term of endearment for the Mother of God in the Greek language.

Paraklitiki: Book based on the weekly cycle of liturgical prayer, containing the hymns of resurrection (for Sundays) as well as hymns for each day of the week (each day of which is dedicated to a different theme: Monday to the angels, Tuesday to St. John the Baptist, Wednesday and Friday to Christ's Cross, Thursday to the Apostles and to St. Nicholas, and Saturday to the martyrs and the reposed).

Pascha: Orthodox Easter.

Pasha: The title of the Ottoman (Turkish) governor of any particular region.

Passionate sympathy: With the sense of the ascetic term "passion." Sympathy that has an element of self-love and selfishness.

Philotimo: A word Elder Paisios was fond of using, for which there is no equivalent in English. According to Elder Paisios's understanding *philotimo*, "is the reverent distillation of goodness, the love shown by humble people, from which every trace of self has been filtered out. Their hearts are full of gratitude towards God and to their fellow men, and out of spiritual sensitivity, they try to repay the slightest good which others do them." [Elder Paisios the Athonite, *Epistles*. Souroti, Greece: Holy Monastery of the Evangelist John the Theologian, 2002, 34].

Phronyma: A Greek word denoting the proper spirit, understanding, etc. of those in the Orthodox Church. Proper phronyma is a natural result of a life lived in the Church.

Prayer, The: It is common in Greece for the Jesus Prayer to be referred to as "the prayer."

Prothesi: The preparation of the bread on the holy prothesi (see below), which will be used for Holy Communion. This preparation takes place before the liturgy begins. As the priest prepares the bread, he says special prayers and commemorates Orthodox Christians, living and reposed.

Prothesi, Holy: A small table to the left of the holy altar where the preparation of the gifts takes place.

Rasaphore: A Greek word meaning "cassock-wearing." It is the second stage in monasticism, after the noviate, during which time the candidate for monasticism is given the blessing to wear the black monastic garb.

Skete: A type of monastic organization somewhere between a coenobitic monastery and a hermitage. In a skete a group of small monastic dwellings are located around a central church. Generally speaking, each dwelling houses one to three monks and operates as an independent unit, except for a certain amount of common life of prayer in the central church, at least on Sundays, but at some sketes more often.

Small Compline: The traditional prayers before bed said by Orthodox Christians (according to Greek practice). In monasteries, the whole community usually reads it after the evening meal.

Stole: See *Epitrahili.*

Supplicatory Canon: A special hymn of supplication to Christ, the Theotokos, a Saint, or the angels. This is one of the many elements of the Church's rich liturgical tradition, which fills up the liturgical day and which may be said by the faithful at any time of need or thanksgiving.

Theotokos: Greek word for the Virgin Mary meaning, literally, "Mother of God."

Three Great Hierarchs: Sts. Basil the Great, Gregory the Theologian, and John Chrysostom.

Tonsure: The action of making a person a monk.

Uncreated Light: The light of Divine Being that appeared to the disciples on Mt. Tabor (Matthew 17:1-9), and that has been experienced by the Church's Saints throughout the history of Christianity. In the fourteenth century, St. Gregory Palamas zealously defended the existential experience of the Uncreated Light, understood to be an Uncreated Energy of God.

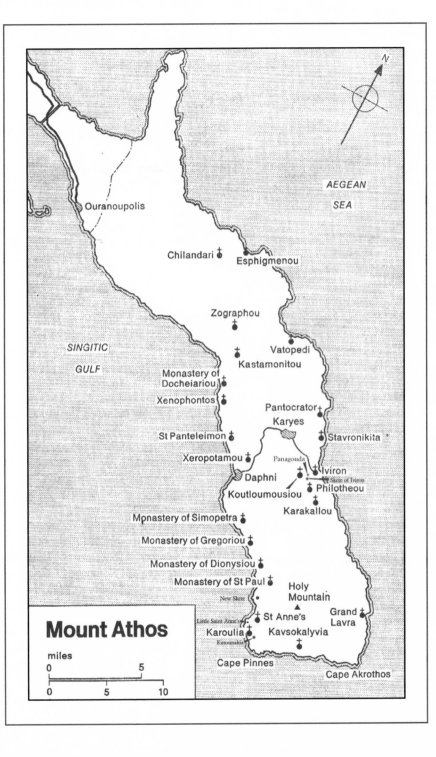

Mount Athos

miles

0		5

| 0 | 5 | 10 |

Ouranoupolis

AEGEAN

SEA

Chilandari ⚲   Esphigmenou

Zographou ⚲

SINGITIC   Vatopedi

GULF   Kastamonitou ✝

Monastery of ✝
Docheiariou ⚲

Xenophontos ⚲

Pantocrator ✝
Karyes

St Panteleimon ⚲   Stavronikita ⚲

Xeropotamou ⚲   Panagouda

Daphni   ✝ Iviron
    Mt Skete of Iviron
Koutloumousiou   Philotheou ✝

Karakallou ✝

Monastery of Simopetra ⚲

Monastery of Gregoriou ⚲

Monastery of Dionysiou ⚲

Monastery of St Paul ⚲   Holy
    Mountain

New Skete   ▲

Little Saint Anne's ✝   St Anne's   Grand ✝
    Lavra

Karoulia ⚲   Kavsokalyvia
Katounakia

Cape Pinnes   Cape Akrothos

N

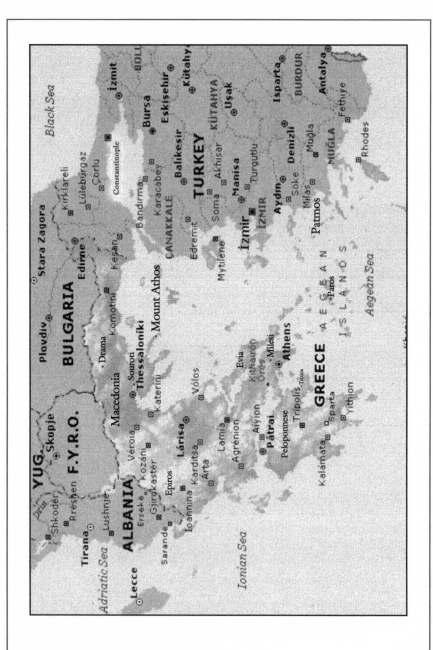

Greece

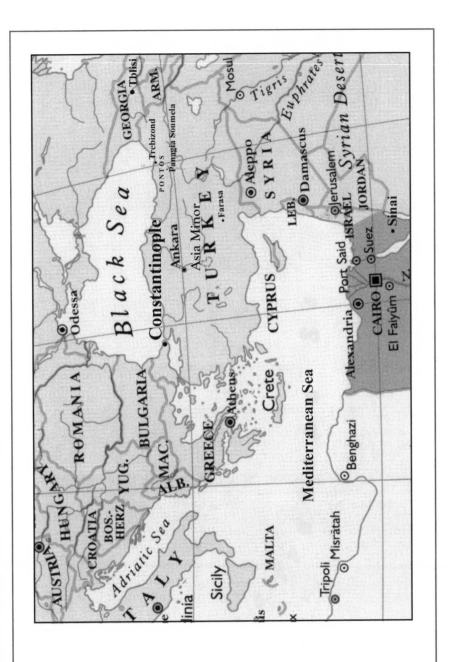

The Eastern Mediterranean

SELECT BIBLIOGRAPHY

In English

Cavarnos, Constantine, *Blessed Elder Philotheos Zervakos.* Belmont, MA: Institute for Byzantine and Modern Greek Studies, 1993.

Christodoulos, Priest-monk, *Elder Paisios: Holy Mountain's Monk.* Mount Athos, Greece.

Holy Coenobium of the Keharitomeni Theotokos, *Counsels For Life: From the Life and Teachings of Fr. Epiphanios Theodoropoulos.* Thessalonica, Greece: Orthodox Kypseli Publications,1995.

Ioannidis, Klitos, *Elder Porphyrios.* Milesi, Greece: Monastery of the Transfiguration.

Joseph, Elder, *Elder Joseph the Hesychast: Struggles, Experiences, Teachings.* Mount Athos, Greece: The Great and Holy Monastery of Vatopaidi, 1999.

Monastic Wisdom: The Letters of Elder Joseph the Hesychast. Florence, AZ: St. Anthony's Greek Monastery, 1998.

Kalymnos, Monastery, *Our Geronda* [Fr. Amphilochios Makris]. Kalymnos, Greece.

Precious Vessels

Moses, Monk, *The Blessed Elder George Karslides (1901-1959)*. Thessalonica, Greece: Orthodox Kypseli Publications, 1998.

Orthodox Kypseli, *The Blessed Elder Philotheos Zervakos*. Thessalonica, Greece: Orthodox Kypseli, 1986.

Papadopoulos S., *The Garden of the Holy Spirit (Elder Iakovos Tsalikis)*. Thessalonica, Greece: Kyriakidis Publications.

Yiannitsiotis, Constantine, *With Elder Porphyrios: A Spiritual Child Remembers*. Athens, Greece: Holy Monastery of the Transfiguration of the Savior, 2001.

In Greek

Αγαπίου, Μοναχού, *Η Θεϊκή Φλόγα (που άναψε στην καρδιά μου), Ο Γέρων Πορφύριος*. Αθήνα, Εκδόσεις Ι. Η. Μεταμορφώσεως του Σωτήρος, 1999.

Αργύρη, Αρχιμ. Ιεροθέου, *Ο Ποιήσας και Διδάξας, Αρχιμανδρίτης Επιφάνιος Θεοδωρόπουλος*. Αθήνα, Εκδόσεις Υπακοής, 2001.

Θεοκλήτου, Μοναχού Διονυσιάτου, *Ο Όσιος Φιλόθεος της Πάρου, Ένας Ένθεος Ασκητής-Ιεραπόστολος (1884-1980)*. Πάρου, Ι. Μ. Παν. Μυρτιδιώτισσας, 1999.

Ι. Μ. Οσίου Δαβίδ του Γέροντος, *Ένας Άγιος Γέροντας, Ο Μακαριστός Π. Ιάκωβος*. Λίμνη, Εύβοια, 1996.

Ι. Η. Κεχαριτωμένης Θεοτόκου, *Υποθήκες Ζωής. Από τη ζωή και τη διδασκαλία του Πατρός Επιφανίου*. Τρoίζηνα, Εκδόσεις Ι. Η. Κεχαριτωμένης Θεοτόκου, 2000.

Ιωαννίδη, Κλείτου, *Ο Γέρων Πορφύριος, Μαρτυρίες και Εμπειρίες*. Αθήνα, Εκδόσεις Ι. Η. Μεταμορφώσεως του Σωτήρος. 1993.

Ιωσήφ, Μοναχού, *Γέρων Ιωσήφ ο Ησυχαστής*. Αγ. Όρος, Εκδόσεις Ι. Μ. Βατοπαιδίου, 2001.

Καλιάτσου, Αναργύρου, *Ο Πατήρ Πορφύριος*. Αθήνα, Εκδόσεις Επταλόφου, 1996.

Κρουσταλάκη, Γ., *Ο Γέρων Πορφύριος, Ο Πνευματικός Πατέρας...*, Αθήνα, Εκδόσεις Ιχνηλασίας, 1997.

Μωϋσέως, Μοναχού Αγιορείτου, *Ο Μακάριος Γέροντας Γεώργιος Καρσλίδης (1901-1959)*. Δράμα, Εκδόσεις Ι. Μ. Αναλήψεως του Σωτήρος, 2002.

Ορθοδόξου Κυψέλης, *Ο Γέρων Φιλόθεος Ζερβάκος*. Θεσσαλονίκη, Εκδόσεις Ορθοδόξου Κυψέλης, 1988.

Τάτση, Διονυσίου (Πρεσβυτέρου), *Διδαχές Γερόντων*. Κόνιτσα, Πρεσβυτέρου Διονυσίου Τάτση, 1996.

Τριάντη, Ιγνατίου Λ. (Μετροπολίτου Βερατίου, Αυλώνος, και Κανίνης), *Ο Γέροντας Της Πάτμου, Αμφιλόχιος Μακρής (1889-1970)*. Πάτμος, Εκδόσεις Ι. Μ. Ευαγγελισμού Μ. Η., 1997.

Χατζόπουλου, Γ. Κ., *Θαύματα και Προφητείες του Οσίου Πατρός Γεωργίου Καρσλίδη*. Δράμα, 1983.

Χατζόπουλου, Γ. Κ., *Γεώργιος Καρσλίδης, ο Θεόπτης και Θεοφόρος Πατήρ*. Δράμα, 1987.

Χατζόπουλου, Γ. Κ. και Διαμαντόπουλου, Ι. Σ., *Η Ζωή και το Έργο του Οσίου Πατρός Γεωργίου Καρσλίδη*.

Χαλή, Ευαγγελίου (Πρεσβυτέρου), *Ο Μακαριστός Γέροντάς Μου, Π. Επιφάνιος Θεοδωρόπουλος*. Αθήνα, Εκδόσεις Νεκταρίου Παναγοπόλου, 2000.

FOR FURTHER READING

Anonymous Russian pilgrim, *The Way of a Pilgrim.*

Chondropoulos, Sotos, *Saint Nektarios: A Saint for our Times.* Brookline, MA: Holy Cross Orthodox Press.

Christensen, Hieromonk Damascene, *Fr. Seraphim Rose: His Life and Works.* Platina, CA: St. Herman of Alaska Brotherhood, 2003.

Cleopa, Elder, *The Truth of Our Faith: Discourses from Holy Scripture on the Tenets of Christian Orthodoxy.* Thessalonica, Greece & London, Ontario: Uncut Mountain Press, 2000.

Florovsky, Georges, *Bible, Church, Tradition: An Eastern Orthodox View.* Belmont, MA: Notable and Academic Books, 1987.

Meyendorff, John, *Byzantine Theology: Historical Trends and Doctrinal Themes.* New York, NY: Fordham University Press, 1983.

Moore, Archimandrite Lazarus, *Saint Seraphim of Sarov, A Spiritual Biography.* New Sarov Press.

Paisios, Elder (of the Holy Mountain), *Saint Arsenios of Cappadocia*. Souroti, Greece: Monastery of St. John the Theologian.

Rose, Fr. Seraphim, *Orthodoxy and the Religion of the Future*. Platina, CA: St. Herman of Alaska Brotherhood.

Rose, Fr. Seraphim, *Saint John the Wonderworker*. Platina, CA: St. Herman of Alaska Brotherhood.

Sakharov, Archimandrite Sophrony, *Saint Silouan the Athonite*. Essex, UK: Stavropegic Monastery of St. John the Baptist, 1991.

Ward, Benedicta, Tr., *The Sayings of the Desert Fathers: The Alphabetical Collection*. Kalamazoo, MI: Cistercian Publications.

Ware, Kallistos, *The Orthodox Church*. London, UK: Penguin Books.

FORTHCOMING FROM

PROTECTING VEIL PRESS

Greece's Dostoevsky
The Theological Vision of
Alexandros Papadiamantis

Professor Anestis Keselopoulos, Ph.D.
Professor of Christian Ethics and Pastoral Theology,
School of Theology, University of Thessalonica

Alexandros Papadiamantis (1851-1911) was the most important literary figure of nineteenth-century Greece and arguably of Modern Greek literature more generally. Through his lively, tender, and profound short stories of the simple lives of the Orthodox faithful of his native island of Skiathos, Papadiamantis reveals a world of organically lived Orthodoxy, largely lost in the disintegrating order of modern life. As with Dostoevsky, Papadiamantis enjoyed close friendships with holy men of his age, such as St. Nicholas Planas. Likewise, as with Dostoevsky, he does not portray a romantic, ideal world. Rather, he presents a profoundly human world of struggle that always, however, has the possibility of transfiguration through life in Christ and His Church. Although wholly unique, the depth and beauty of his writings and of his Orthodox faith make comparisons with Dostoevsky unavoidable.

For many decades overlooked and largely rejected by the Academy, Papadia-mantis's work is finally coming into its own.

With great warmth and sympathy Dr. Keselopoulos provides the first serious attempt to plumb the theological depths of the riches of Papadiamantis.

Dr. Keselopoulos's chief concern is Papadiamantis's description of the liturgical life of Skiathos, which he shows to be an authentic expression of Orthodox faith and piety.

The book is divided into six sections, beginning with an introduction to Papadiamantis's life, world, and work, which provide context for the reader unfamiliar with Papadiamantis. This is followed by a study of Orthodox faith and life that uses Papadiamantis's stories as a vantage point from which to study different aspects of the Church and the faith: clergy (pastoral service, education), the role of lay people (clergy/laity relations, lay people as concelebrators), the tradition of the Church (Biblical tradition as liturgical tradition, Eastern and Western traditions, diachronicity in tradition), liturgical order—typicon (influences from the monastic typicon, liturgical precision and Economy, form and essence in worship), art in worship (the meaning of liturgical art, the museumification of liturgical art), and so on.

Precious Vessels of the Holy Spirit
was typeset in Baskerville Old Face by Protecting Veil Press in
this second edition

GLORY BE TO GOD FOR ALL THINGS. AMEN.